AF544729

BATTLE OF THE

River Plate

SEA BATTLES IN CLOSE-UP · 4

BATTLE OF THE *River Plate*

GEOFFREY BENNETT

This book is published and distributed in the United States by the

UNITED STATES NAVAL INSTITUTE
Annapolis, Maryland 21402

First published 1972

SBN 7110 0280 0

Published by Ian Allan Ltd, Shepperton, Surrey and printed in the United Kingdom by Morrison and Gibb Ltd, London and Edinburgh

Contents

DIAGRAMS

Preface and Acknowledgements

For his prime task, to watch Toulon throughout the year 1804 so that the French fleet might not escape to sea without being brought to battle, Nelson needed all the ships-of-the-line that the Admiralty could give him. To protect Britain's maritime trade flowing in and out of the Mediterranean past the Rock of Gibraltar, he could spare only three 32-gunned frigates. Their commander, Captain John Gore's chief concern was the threat presented by a single French ship-of-the-line, the 74-gunned *Aigle* based on the nearby Spanish port of Cadiz. Yet Nelson, writing from the *Victory*, advised him:

> 'Your intentions of attacking that ship are . . . very laudable, but I do not consider your force by any means equal to it.'

Such caution must seem foreign to a man who had risked his career to ensure a British triumph at the battle of Cape St Vincent (1787) by wearing the *Captain* out of line contrary to the Admiralty's *Fighting Instructions*; who had accepted the navigational hazards of Aboukir Bay and the risks inherent in a night action to ensure the destruction of Brueys' fleet at the battle of the Nile (1798); and who had gained a comparable victory off Copenhagen (1801) by 'turning a blind eye' to his apprehensive Commander-in-Chief's signal of recall. But, like Hawke, Howe, and other great commanders of the age of fighting sail, Nelson judged that a single ship-of-the-line, mounting at least twice as many guns as the majority of frigates, was more than a match for a squadron of three small 'cruisers'.

And this was still the accepted view in the Dreadnought era a century later. In 1914 Rear-Admiral Troubridge, commanding a squadron of four British armoured cruisers bristling with a total of twenty-two 9·2in, fourteen 7·5in and twenty 6in guns, was charged with failing to bring the German battle-cruiser *Goeben*, armed with ten 11in, to action, with disastrous consequences to the Allied cause. But the court martial decided that he 'was justified in considering the *Goeben* a superior force . . . and in abandoning the chase'.

This dogma was nonetheless false. Troubridge could have challenged the *Goeben* with a fair chance of success had he split his force and attacked from two or more different bearings simultaneously. But not until World War II was this proved to be so when Commodore Henry Harwood, with the *Achilles*, *Ajax* and *Exeter*, fought the *Admiral Graf Spee* off the River Plate on December 13, 1939. To quote from a letter written by the First Sea Lord, Admiral Sir Dudley Pound:

> 'Your action . . . has reversed the findings of the Troubridge court martial and shows how wrong that was.'

As with others in this series, Part I of this book tells the story of how these three British cruisers, armed with 8in and 6in guns, not only accepted action with a German pocket-battleship mounting 11in weapons, but drove her to seek refuge in neutral waters where she was scuttled by her crew. This account is preceded by an outline of the events leading up to the battle, and is followed in Part II by a series of appendices listing the ships involved and giving technical data and other relevant facts.

For help in compiling this monograph, with its numerous photographs, diagrams and other illustrations, I am much indebted to Lieutenant-Commander M. E. Holloway, Royal Navy, and to Douglas Robinson, MD, of Pennington, New Jersey, and to the staff of the Imperial War Museum (IWM). I also thank the Radio Times Hulton Picture Library (RTHPL), United Press International (UPI), the Bundesarchiv Militärarchiv Freiburg (BMF) and the Bibliothek für Zeitgeschichte Weltkriegsbücherie, Stuttgart (BZWS) for the loan of photographs.

PART ONE

The Battle

Introduction

The German Navy after World War I

The Peace Treaty signed at Versailles in June 1919, left Germany with only a minuscule Navy; eight pre-dreadnought battleships, eight obsolescent cruisers, 32 destroyers and torpedoboats, and *no* submarines, with personnel limited to 15000 officers and men. And these numbers were not to be exceeded: new construction was restricted to replacements; battleships of only 10000 tons and cruisers of 6000 tons when the existing ones were 20 years old; destroyers and torpedoboats of 600 and 200 tons when the present ones were 15 years old. But this small fleet inherited two invaluable lessons from World War I. On the one hand, Grand Admiral von Tirpitz's much vaunted High Seas Fleet had been proved impotent as a weapon to prevent Britain's Grand Fleet maintaining a blockade of the North Sea that played a large part in Germany's ultimate defeat. On the other hand, Britain had been brought near to defeat by unrestricted U-boat warfare against seaborne trade in the waters round the British Isles and in the Mediterranean, supported further overseas by a similar campaign by a handful of surface raiders.

These two lessons dominated Germany's post-Versailles naval plans, more especially after 1929 when Admiral Erich Raeder became head of the *Reichmarine*. He had fought at Jutland, on Admiral Hipper's staff in the battle-cruiser *Lützow*, and had seen the sequel to that action, the collapse of morale to the point of mutiny in the summer of 1917, and again in November 1918. Later he had written the first volume of *Der Krieg zur See, 1914–19* (the German official history of the naval side of World War I), dealing with cruiser warfare, so that he knew the disproportionate extent to which the few German warships which operated overseas—those which were already there in 1914—had disrupted British trade, notably the *Emden*, under Captain Karl von Müller, during her short career as a marauder in the Indian Ocean. As clear were the small results achieved by the vessels sent out to replace these warships after they had been sunk or otherwise destroyed by British forces—for which Germany had used merchantmen converted to auxiliary cruisers, as much because von Tirpitz had designed his capital ships and most of his cruisers with an endurance that limited them to operating in the North and Baltic Seas, as because their disguise gave them a better chance of eluding the Grand Fleet's patrols.

Recognising that an effective Navy able to profit from these lessons could not be built within the terms of the Versailles Treaty, Germany contrived secretly and skilfully to violate them. As early as 1922 a submarine construction office was established at The Hague under cover of a Dutch firm. In 1928 the prototype of a new class of U-boat was built in Spain, followed in 1930 by another in Finland. In this way, by the end of 1932 Germany was ready to order the first 16 of a new U-boat force. Similarly, and in the context of this book more important, with Germany's surface warships. The first cruiser replacement, completed in 1926 and significantly named *Emden*, was designed for extensive operations overseas. So, too, were her four successors.

By accepting guns of 5·9in calibre, these were built within Treaty limits, but the battleship replacements were a different story. Since it was impossible to design a vessel comparable with a British dreadnought within the Treaty limit of 10000 tons, Germany conceived the *Panzerschiff* (*i.e.* armoured ship), which was soon translated as 'pocket-battleship'. Even so, the *Deutschland*, completed in 1933, followed by her two sisters; the *Admiral Scheer* named after the C-in-C of the High Seas Fleet at Jutland, in 1934; and the *Admiral Graf Spee*, named after the victor of Coronel (November 1, 1914) whose Far East Squadron was subsequently annihilated at the Falkland Islands (December 8, 1914), early in 1936; had a standard displacement of 12100 tons and a full-load of as much as 16200 tons. Each armed with six 11in guns, these were not only protected by armour able to withstand the impact of an 8in gunned cruiser's shells, but equipped with diesel machinery which gave them a cruising radius of 19000 miles and a maximum speed of 26 knots.* And their significance lay not only in their obvious rôle as commerce raiders, but the fact that, of Britain's capital ships, *i.e.* ships with guns of larger calibre than 8in, only three, the battle-cruisers *Hood*, *Renown* and *Repulse*, had the speed to catch them; and of France's

* For fuller details of the *Admiral Graf Spee* and *Deutschland*, see Appendix 8.

none until she completed the battle-cruisers *Dunkerque* and *Strasbourg* shortly before 1939.

Raeder's need to build U-boats in secret, and to construct nothing larger than pocket-battleships and light cruisers, ended when Hitler seized power. After the Treaty of Versailles had been publicly repudiated in March 1935, the Anglo-German Naval Agreement, signed three months later, restricted him only to a total surface tonnage not exceeding 35 per cent of the British, and parity in submarine tonnage. On Hitler's assurance that war was unlikely before 1944, Raeder then initiated the construction of two battle-cruisers, two battleships, an aircraft carrier and five 8in gunned cruisers. And when the Anglo-German agreement was unilaterally abrogated in April 1939, he went on to plan the production of a balanced fleet of 13 capital ships, four aircraft carriers, 33 cruisers and as many as 250 U-boats by 1945.

These plans were, however, set at nought by Hitler's impatience. The rape of Czecho-Slovakia, followed by Germany's *blitzkrieg* attack on Poland, provoked war with Britain and France in September 1939, when only three of these new surface ships were ready; the battle-cruisers *Scharnhorst* and *Gneisenau* (which had been kept within the Washington Treaty limit of 35000 tons by arming them with nine 11in guns as compared with the *Hood*'s eight 15in, the *Renown* and *Repulse*'s six of this larger calibre, and the *Dunkerque*'s and *Strasbourg*'s eight 12in), and the 8in cruiser *Admiral Hipper* (which exceeded the Washington Treaty limit of 10000 tons by nearly 5000 so that she was half as big again as her British and French counterparts).

Germany's War Plans

Against the British Commonwealth's 15 capital ships, six aircraft carriers, 15 8in and 48 6in cruisers, plus France's five capital ships, two aircraft carriers and 15 8in and 6in cruisers, Raeder could oppose little more than two battle-cruisers, three pocket-battleships and six cruisers. He had, moreover, only enough U-boats to keep some ten on patrol at any one time. How, then, was Germany to wage war at sea until such time as this minuscule, but now largely modern Fleet could be reinforced by new construction, and by the conversion of merchant ships into more formidable auxiliary cruisers than those of World War I?

The *Reichmarine's Battle Instructions*, issued in May 1939, supposed that Germany would have to fight a war on two fronts, against Britain and France in the west, and against Poland and Russia in the east. The latter need was, however, largely eliminated by the Russo-German pact signed in August 1939. The German Fleet's prime tasks were the protection of its own coasts; the defence of its own, and attack on the enemy's, sea communications in the North and Baltic Seas, to the limited extent that this might be possible in the face of a much stronger British Fleet; the support of land operations in these areas; and to act as a 'politico-strategic instrument' to ensure the neutrality of the Scandinavian countries. For all this Raeder had to allocate the great majority of his ships, dividing them into a main force based on Wilhelmshaven for operations in the North Sea, and a smaller one on Kiel for operations in the Baltic.

For the German Fleet's secondary task, 'war on merchant shipping', Raeder could spare only its U-boats, whose range restricted them to waters round the British Isles—and two pocket-battleships. These potentially powerful raiders were to be sailed secretly before the outbreak of war. So, too, were supply ships which should enable them to remain at large for many months before they were compelled to run the gauntlet of the British Fleet in order to return to Germany. Their task was 'disruption and destruction of enemy merchant shipping by all possible means', chiefly in the North and South Atlantic, by 'making sudden appearances in widely separated areas', followed by 'withdrawal into the ocean wastes'. They were not to seek 'combat even against inferior enemy naval forces . . . [since] even slight damage can decrease their effectiveness and cruising endurance'. When attacking merchant ships they were to observe the Hague Convention governing war at sea—but only 'for the present'. The likely need to adopt unrestricted war on merchant shipping to achieve decisive results, especially by U-boats, was foreseen in the sentence:

> 'It goes without saying that effective . . . fighting methods will never fail to be employed merely because some international regulations . . . are opposed to them.'

Britain's War Plans

The Admiralty's war plans had to make the best possible use of a Fleet constricted by American ambitions, economic difficulties, and by the Washington and London Naval Treaties, to a mere shadow of the force with which Britain had ruled the seas in 1914–18. Those issued in January 1939 had nonetheless to envisage a conflict between, on the one side, Britain and France, without American support, and, on the other, Germany and Italy, with the possibility of subsequent intervention by Japan.

The largest British force, which included seven battleships, three battle-cruisers and four aircraft carriers was, as always, allocated to Home waters. Its manifold tasks included establishing an effective blockade of Germany, combating any offensive operations by her Fleet, notably preventing the egress of surface raiders, and protecting seaborne trade in the Western Approaches and in coastal waters. The French having undertaken to deal with the Italian Fleet in the western half of the Mediterranean, Britain intended to counter it in the eastern half with her other three capital ships (two being in dockyard's hands for modernisation) and one aircraft carrier, with the reservation that, in the event of Japan entering the war, this force would have to proceed through the Suez Canal to the Far East.

Seaborne trade was to be protected in two ways. In Home waters, where U-boats might be active, albeit on a small scale, merchant ships would be sailed in escorted convoys. Unlike World War I, the value of these as a defensive-offensive measure was fully recognised. Troopships, too, especially those crossing the Atlantic from Canada, would be sailed in ocean convoys with capital ship or cruiser escort. But the great majority of Britain's merchant ships—on average 2500 at sea on any one day, steaming along the many thousands of miles of highly vulnerable ocean sea routes which were 'vital to the life of the Empire'—could be given only such limited protection, against sporadic attacks by enemy raiders, as might be afforded by a world-wide dispersal of the few cruisers available after providing for the essential needs of Home and Mediterranean waters. These numbered seven in the North Atlantic, eight in the South (of which three formed the South American Division), three in the Indian Ocean, four plus an aircraft carrier on the China Station, and seven in Australian and New Zealand waters. And who could say how successful these would be if, as was expected, Germany employed her pocket-battleships as ocean raiders? To quote the words of the First Sea Lord, Admiral Sir Dudley Pound, to the British Chiefs of Staffs:

> 'Nothing could paralyse our supply system and seaborne trade so certainly and immediately as a successful attack by surface raiders.'

Fortunately, France, in addition to allocating three battleships and an aircraft carrier to her sphere of the Mediterranean, intended to base a *Force de Raid* of two battle-cruisers and an aircraft carrier on Brest, to operate against German raiders in the area where they could be most dangerous, the North Atlantic.

August 1939

As war loomed large in the summer of 1939, Britain and France mobilised their reserves in time to deploy their Fleets in accordance with these plans (*see Appendices 2 and 3*). So, too, did Germany (*see Appendix 4*). Of the Italian and Japanese Fleets nothing need be said except that the bulk of the former stayed in its own waters, and that the latter likewise adhered to its own and Chinese waters; because, in the event, neither ventured to open hostilities against Britain until after the period covered by this book, with the important consequence that the Admiralty was able to withdraw ships temporarily from both the Mediterranean and the eastern oceans for service elsewhere.

Few of the movements required to effect these dispositions need comment. In mid-August HMS *Cumberland* left the Home Fleet to join the South American Division; the Australian Navy's *Perth* sailed to reinforce the American and West Indies Squadron; the New Zealand Navy's *Achilles* sailed for Valparaiso; and four old cruisers from the Reserve Fleet sailed to join HMS *Neptune* in the South Atlantic. Much more important, however, on August 21 the *Admiral Graf Spee* left Wilhelmshaven, followed three days later by the *Deutschland* And by keeping close to the Danish and Norwegian coasts until they were far to the north, and by making best use of the available hours of darkness, both pocket-battleships passed north of the Faroes and headed for their war stations without being reported.

It is arguable that in this achievement luck was on the side of the *Admiral Graf Spee*'s commander, the able 45-year-old Captain Hans Langsdorff. Had he sailed one day earlier he must have been spotted by RAF Coastal Command who, from August 15 to 20, flew extensive patrols across the North Sea as part of a major exercise carried out by the Home Fleet. Ironically enough, this was designed to practise British ships and aircraft in their war task of intercepting German raiders trying to break out into the Atlantic. But, to judge by the poor performance of these patrols—due to insufficient training in ship recognition, their observers were frequently unable to distinguish between ships so different in size as a battle-cruiser and a destroyer—it is also arguable that, had they been flying on, say, August 22, the chances are that they would not have spotted and reported the *Admiral Graf Spee* with any degree of credibility.

The German naval auxiliary tanker *Altmark*, commanded by the ageing Captain Heinrich Dau, which was destined to keep the *Graf Spee* supplied with fuel, had preceded the pocket-battleship. So, too, had the *Westerwald* which was to partner the *Deutschland*. The *Altmark** had, indeed, passed down Channel openly as early as August 6, bound for Port Arthur, Texas, where she filled her tanks before heading for her first rendezvous with the *Graf Spee*.

* For details see Appendix 6.

CHAPTER ONE

The Cruise of the Admiral Graf Spee

Preliminary Moves, August 21 to September 25, 1939

Carrying a crew of 1124 officers and men, the *Admiral Graf Spee* steered to pass between the Faeroes and Iceland on August 24.* Captain Langsdorff then headed south, timing his passage to cross the main Atlantic shipping lanes at night, for a position northwest of the Azores. Here on the 28th he met the *Altmark* and topped up with fuel before the two ships continued their voyage in company. On September 3, the day that Britain and France declared war, pocket-battleship and supply ship were to the west of the Cape Verde Islands. And still keeping clear of all regular shipping routes, they crossed the Equator on September 8 to reach an area in the middle of the South Atlantic seldom frequented by shipping on September 13 without being reported.

In this achievement Langsdorff was again lucky. Two days earlier, the *Graf Spee*'s Arado seaplane, on a reconnaissance flight, had sighted HMS *Cumberland* proceeding from Freetown to Rio de Janeiro, on an approaching course. And, because the weather was fair and the visibility extreme, the German aircraft was able to warn Langsdorff and Dau to alter course to the eastward, and slip away from an enemy with whom neither had any wish to be engaged, without itself being sighted by the British cruiser.

The *Deutschland*, though she sailed three days after the *Graf Spee* and took a longer route to the north of Iceland, and through the Denmark Straits on August 28, had meantime reached an area immediately to the south of Greenland by the end of that month.

If Admiral Raeder had had his own way, both pocket-battleships would have begun making their, to him, vital contribution to

* For a chronological summary of events from this date onwards, see Appendix 1.

Diagram 1. The cruise of the *Admiral Graf Spee*, August 21–December 13, 1939

Germany's maritime war as soon as September 3. But Hitler withheld his permission in the vain hope that, having quickly conquered Poland without Britain and France being able to intervene, these two countries would make peace. On September 5 both captains received strict instructions to stay clear of all shipping until further orders. So the *Graf Spee* remained in her waiting area, to the north of the Plate–Cape of Good Hope trade route, to the east of the Plate–UK route and to the west of the Cape–UK route, inactive, except for refuelling twice from the *Altmark*, on the 13th and the 20th, and unseen, no more than a phantom foe. And the *Deutschland* remained in her waiting area clear of the North Atlantic trade routes, likewise unseen and inactive, except for occasionally refuelling from the *Westerwald*.

Not until September 26 were both pocket-battleships at last unleashed to begin 'the disruption and destruction of enemy merchant shipping by all possible means'. Even so their captains had to observe several restrictions. In the vain hope that it might help to divide France from Britain, Hitler enforced another three weeks delay before they were allowed to attack French, as well as British, merchant ships. Furthermore, both captains were warned that, on September 5, President Roosevelt had declared a Pan-American Neutrality Zone extending 300 to 600 miles from the east coasts of North and South America. This was patrolled by the US Navy so as to discourage the belligerents from conducting hostile operations which might hazard merchant ships, especially those flying the US flag, on the routes up and down the coasts of the USA and of South America, and in the Caribbean. Langsdorff and his brother raider were therefore instructed to avoid incidents which might alienate US opinion. They were not, however, forbidden to operate within this Neutrality Zone, for which there was no precedent in International Law; nor did the British and French Governments concede that it placed any restriction on the rights of their ships to pursue and engage the enemy within it. For the same reason—Hitler's desire to placate US opinion—Raeder was obliged to remind the *Graf Spee* and the *Deutschland* that they were to conduct their campaign in accordance with International Prize Law, even when this restriction was progressively lifted from his U-boats, following *U-30*'s successful torpedo attack on the British passenger liner *Athenia* as early as September 3 in the misguided belief that she was an armed merchant-cruiser.

The Cruise of the Deutschland and Other German Naval Operations, September 26 to November 26, 1939

The stories of the *Deutschland*'s first brief career as a raider, and of two other significant operations by the German Navy, are best told before dealing further with the *Graf Spee*, because of their impact on British and French countermeasures against her. On September 27 the *Deutschland* headed south in search of prey in the North Atlantic, to find her first victim, the ss *Stonegate*, on October 5, 600 miles to the east of Bermuda. Since this British freighter managed to transmit a distress message before she was sunk, her assailant immediately left the area. Heading north she intercepted the US freighter *City of Flint* and, finding that she carried a cargo for Britain, put a prize crew onboard with orders to head for the Soviet port of Murmansk. Next, on the 14th, the *Deutschland* sank the Norwegian freighter *Lorenz W. Hansen* to the east of Newfoundland. Two neutrals out of a total of only three victims in as many weeks! This was more likely to turn neutral opinion against Germany than affect Britain's war effort. Before she could do any further damage, or be at risk to British forces which must by now be hunting for her, the *Deutschland* was recalled to Germany.

Passing back through the Denmark Straits on the 8th, and heading far to the north, she turned down for the Norwegian coast on the 11th, reached the Skagerrak without being spotted by the patrols of RAF Coastal Command on the 14th, and next day entered the Baltic port of Gotenhafen. But she continued to absorb the attentions of both the Admiralty and the C-in-C Home Fleet, Admiral Sir Charles Forbes, for another month, because not until mid-December did they know that this pocket-battleship and the *Westerwald* had returned to Germany.

During this period Forbes had to contend with two other significant moves by German surface forces. In order to discourage the Admiralty from detaching Home Fleet units to help search for his pocket-battleships (albeit to little effect as will be seen in the next chapter), Raeder ordered the battle-cruiser *Gneisenau*, accompanied by the cruiser *Köln* and nine destroyers, to make a brief sortie. At 1320 on October 8 they were seen and reported off Lister Light by an aircraft of Coastal Command. The Home Fleet immediately put to sea. Rightly assuming, because this was the greatest danger, that the principal units of this enemy force intended to break out into the Atlantic and operate against trade, Forbes disposed his ships to intercept it, across to the Norwegian coast and to the north of the Shetlands, moves with which Coastal Command confirmed. But the German commander was under orders to proceed no further than the southwest coast of Norway, attacking any light forces and merchant shipping he might find there. The almost inevitable consequence was that the British, having lost touch with the enemy force off Stavanger at 1730 on the 8th, failed to find it again on the 9th, or before it re-entered the Kattegat at noon on the 10th.

The second German operation was potentially more dangerous. On November 21 the battle-cruisers *Gneisenau* and *Scharnhorst* sailed from Wilhelmshaven, intending to break out through the Iceland–Faeroes gap for a brief feint against the North Atlantic trade routes, designed to dislocate them, and to draw off ships searching for the *Graf Spee*, before slipping home again at high speed. But not all went according to Raeder's plan. Although both battle-cruisers steamed up the Norwegian coast and passed north of the Faeroes without being spotted, in the Iceland–Faeroes passage soon after 1530 on November 23 they ran into HMS *Rawalpindi*. This P & O liner was one of several such ships converted into armed merchant-cruisers to augment the Home Fleet's Northern Patrol.

Hopelessly outclassed by two more heavily gunned and armoured ships from which she lacked the speed to fly, the *Rawalpindi* fought with a gallantry that gained Captain E. C. Kennedy a posthumous VC after she was sunk in a one-sided action that lasted for less than a quarter of an hour. But neither Kennedy nor his crew gave their lives in vain. In that short period the *Rawalpindi* radioed two enemy reports, both unfortunately misleading, the first of *one* battle-cruiser, the second correcting this to read *Deutschland*. Forbes immediately ordered his fleet to intercept; the *Nelson*, *Rodney* and *Devonshire* from the Clyde, the *Aurora*, *Edinburgh* and *Southampton* from Rosyth, the *Newcastle*, five 'C' and one 'D' class cruiser from the Faeroes–Iceland patrol, the *Norfolk* and *Suffolk* from the Denmark Strait, the *Sheffield* and three 'D' class cruisers from Loch Ewe, the *Glasgow* from escorting a Norwegian convoy which was recalled to the Forth. As quickly the Admiralty detached the *Warspite* from escorting a Halifax convoy to the Denmark Strait, ordered the *Hood* to leave Plymouth and join the French *Dunkerque*, and the *Repulse* and *Furious* to sail from Halifax, these four ships to cover the North Atlantic trade routes.

The *Newcastle*, next on the patrol line to the *Rawalpindi*, altered course to close her position at full speed as soon as she received her enemy reports. Two hours later she sighted both enemy battle-cruisers stopped and recovering survivors from the *Rawalpindi*, a fortunate 39. For no good reason, instead of engaging this single British cruiser, the two German ships made off to the east. The *Newcastle* attempted to follow and shadow but was foiled by a rainstorm: when the visibility cleared soon after 1830, the enemy had disappeared into the darkness. And neither she, nor the *Delhi* which joined her, managed to regain touch during the night.

The German Admiral Marschall realised that, since his position had been reported, the British would use intensive aircraft patrols to relocate him, and move every available warship in his direction. So he decided on a speedy return to Germany rather than continuing his feint against the trade routes, even though the few British and French ships—five in all—which could engage him on equal terms were many hundreds of miles from his position. By the 24th the German battle-cruisers were well to the north of Norway: on the 25th they turned south for the North Sea: by the 26th they were 20 miles to the west of Statlandet, without having been sighted by any of the numerous British warships and aircraft which were searching for them.

And Marschall's luck held. By that day Forbes had a dozen cruisers only eight miles apart on a patrol line stretching west from the Norwegian coast towards the Shetlands. But although the Germans sighted one of these cruisers as they passed through this line during the night of the 26th, they were not themselves seen. And thereafter, in worsening weather which was to their advantage, Marschall's ships reached the safety of Wilhelmshaven at 1300 on November 27, leaving the Home Fleet to continue a fruitless search until December 1 before Forbes received this unpalatable intelligence and returned to port.

To be fair, Marschall enjoyed one important advantage, a radio intelligence service in Berlin which gave him advance warning of Forbes's dispositions and movements. Not until well into 1940 did the British realise how easily their ciphers were being broken by the Germans and introduce new ones that were more secure. And Forbes suffered the further handicap of having no aircraft carriers in his fleet. The *Courageous* had fallen a victim to *U-29* as early as September 17: the *Ark Royal*, *Furious* and *Hermes* had been ordered overseas, to help in the search for the *Deutschland* and the *Admiral Graf Spee*.

The Cruise of the Admiral Graf Spee, September 26 to December 12

As soon as he was released by Berlin on September 26, Langsdorff headed the *Admiral Graf Spee* for the coast of Brazil. He could do no greater damage than disrupt Britain's meat and grain imports from the Argentine which, flowing north from Buenos Aires, must pass close off Pernambuco. So it was in a position 75 miles southeast of this port (and despite the Pan-American Neutrality Zone) that, shortly before noon on the 30th, he found his first victim, the ss *Clement*, a veteran 5051-ton tramp belonging to the Booth Line. Machine-gun bullets sprayed around his bridge by the *Graf Spee*'s seaplane were enough to dispel Captain F. C. P. Harris's belief that the approaching warship was HMS *Ajax*. Having stopped engines and instructed his radio operator to transmit a distress message, he ordered his crew to abandon ship.

When all had taken to the boats, Langsdorff sank the *Clement* by gunfire—five rounds of 11in and 25 of 5·9in. Since the sea was calm he took Harris and his chief engineer onboard the *Graf Spee*, the first for questioning, the second to have a wounded hand attended to, before transferring both to a passing Greek steamer, the ss *Papelemos*, after extracting a promise from her captain that he would make no W/T* report, which he kept until he reached St Vincent in the Cape Verde Islands on October 9. The rest of the crew, in their boats, were given the course to steer for the South American coast. One load of 13 survivors was soon picked up by the Brazilian ss *Itatinga* and landed at Maceio on October 1; the other boats reached this Brazilian port next day.

Knowing that the alarm had been given by the *Clement*, with the consequent likelihood of British warships being drawn to the Pernambuco area, Langsdorff sped the *Graf Spee* eastwards at 18 knots for a very different part of the South Atlantic, intending to disrupt another trade route, that between the Cape of Good Hope and Europe. There, early on October 5, he found the ss *Newton Beech*, a British tramp of 4651 tons carrying a cargo of maize. Captain J. Robinson's radio operator managed to transmit a distress message before Langsdorff could put a prize crew aboard; and this was intercepted by another British merchant ship which, later in the day, fell in with HMS *Cumberland* and passed it to her. Had Captain W. H. G. Fallowfield transmitted it to the C-in-C South Atlantic at Freetown,

* Wireless telegraphy.

Admiral Sir D'Oyly Lyon, the chances are that the *Graf Spee* would have been rounded up within the week. But Fallowfield was chiefly concerned to avoid revealing his own ship's presence in the area: rather than break W/T silence, he made the faulty assumption that the *Newton Beech*'s message must have been received by the W/T station at Freetown.

Captain Dau was as lucky four days later: on October 9 the *Altmark* was sighted to the southwest of the Cape Verde Islands by aircraft from HMS *Ark Royal*, Captain A. J. Power. By claiming that his ship was the American ss *Delmar*, Dau dissuaded the Vice-Admiral Aircraft Carriers, L. V. Wells, against taking his flagship some distance off her course for Freetown in order to test the truth of this. Not until much later did he and Power learn that the *Delmar* was in New Orleans on this date.

Keeping the *Newton Beech* with him for the time being, Langsdorff headed the *Graf Spee* further east and early on October 7 surprised the 4222-ton British cargo steamer *Ashlea*, carrying a cargo of crude sugar. She was boarded before Captain C. Pottinger realised that his ship was being seized by the enemy, so that her radio operator had no chance to transmit a distress message. For the same reason Pottinger failed to destroy his confidential Admiralty instructions from which Langsdorff gained useful intelligence, just as he had already done from the *Newton Beech*. The *Ashlea*'s crew having been transferred to the *Newton Beech*, she was sunk by scuttling charges. Two days later Langsdorff decided against keeping the *Newton Beech* for any longer; having transferred her crew and the *Ashlea*'s to the *Altmark*, she too was scuttled.

Twenty-four hours more, and on the evening of October 10 the *Graf Spee* found her fourth victim, the 8196-ton liner *Huntsman*, on passage from Calcutta to London, via the Cape, with a cargo of tea. Like Coppinger of the *Ashlea*, Captain A. H. Brown allowed the *Graf Spee* to close, under the impression that she was an Allied vessel, until a signal threatening to sink the *Huntsman* by gun fire if she transmitted a distress message, sufficed to dissuade him from hazarding the lives of his crew. So the presence of the *Graf Spee* on the Cape–UK trade route went unreported as Langsdorff returned to his waiting area, followed by the *Huntsman* with a prize crew on board.

In this safe zone the *Graf Spee* refuelled from the *Altmark*. Two days later, and as with the *Newton Beech*, Langsdorff accepted the impracticability of sailing the *Huntsman* through the British Home Fleet's blockade back to Germany with a prize crew aboard. Her captain having been transferred to the *Graf Spee* and the rest of her crew to Dau's supply ship, she was scuttled.

Langsdorff was now in possession of a copy of the secret code supplied by the Admiralty to British merchant ships. With the advantage of intelligence thus gained from intercepted W/T traffic, he decided to make another foray against the Cape–UK trade route, but further to the south. On October 22, he sighted the 5299-ton British ss *Trevanion* homeward bound from Port Pirie with 8000 tons of concentrates. Although Captain J. M. Edwards was misled by the *Graf Spee*'s French flag into allowing her to close well inside a mile before he realised that she was a pocket-battleship, his radio operator managed to transmit a report despite the machine-gun fire aimed at the bridge and wireless office which this provoked. The *Trevanion* was then boarded and scuttled after Edwards and his crew had been taken aboard the *Graf Spee*. But they had already done their duty well; their distress message had been picked up by the liner *Llanstephen Castle* and immediately relayed to Freetown.

Realising that he was now in considerable danger of being trapped by British warships, Langsdorff made a wise decision. Having returned to his waiting area to refuel again from the *Altmark* on October 29, and to transfer his latest batch of prisoners, he acted on a suggestion signalled by Raeder from Berlin. Heading southeast, the *Graf Spee* steamed more than 3000 miles, passing far to the south of the Cape of Good Hope on November 3, and entered the Indian Ocean. En route Langsdorff learned that 100 Iron Crosses had been awarded to his crew.

But ten days of slow cruising on the Cape–Australia trade route produced no prey: the wool clip was late this year and ships carrying it to Britain had not yet left Australian ports. So Langsdorff turned north for the Mozambique Channel, between Madagascar and the African continent, where, on the 15th off Lourenço Marques, he sighted the small 706-ton tanker ss *Africa Shell* in ballast. Captain P. Dove was taken by surprise and boarded before he could transmit a distress message, He and his crew having been taken aboard the *Graf Spee*, his ship was sunk.

Next day Langsdorff sighted another vessel, only to find that she was the Dutch ss *Mapia*. Respecting her neutrality he allowed her to go. He then judged that he had done enough to alert the enemy to his presence in the Indian Ocean. The *Africa Shell* would soon be reported overdue; the Dutch captain would report their encounter when he reached Sumatra. So the *Graf Spee* turned south, to pass again through the Roaring Forties on November 20, and to reach her South Atlantic waiting area on the 23rd. There Langsdorff spent four days overhauling his ship's engines, disguising her to resemble HMS *Renown* by erecting an additional turret and funnel of wood and canvas,* and making a fateful decision, which he recorded in a nine-page memorandum saying, *inter alia*:

> 'The *Graf Spee*, having now steamed 30000 miles, should continue to cause damage and disruption to enemy shipping for as long as possible in order to tie down the greatest possible enemy forces in defence of trade. [But her] machinery requires a dockyard overhaul in the near future. The period of commerce raiding is therefore nearing an end, and in consequence, the necessity for avoiding action damage no longer so pressing. If the *Graf Spee* was to close the range her powerful armament should at least so damage an opponent as to eliminate him as a shadower. The *Graf Spee* will, therefore, operate again on the Cape route until about December 6. As soon as it is clear that the enemy has been alarmed, the *Graf Spee* will cross the South Atlantic and operate against the River Plate traffic, before returning to Germany in the New Year.'

Accordingly, on the 26th, the *Graf Spee* refuelled, stored and provisioned from the *Altmark*, and Langsdorff redistributed his prisoners. The captains, first officers, radio officers and chief engineers from his victims were transferred to the *Graf Spee* so that they might be taken back to Germany. Their crews, for whom there was no room onboard the pocket-battleship, were left in the *Altmark*, Dau being given orders to land them at some neutral port.

This done, Langsdorff headed for the Cape–UK route where, at midday on December 2, he sighted the 10086-ton Blue Star liner *Doric Star*, homeward bound from New Zealand and Australia with 8000 tons of mutton, butter, cheese and wool. This time he made no use of his disguise to surprise his victim; instead he opened fire at

* In addition to this disguise, and the use of French colours to enable the *Graf Spee* to close her victims before they recognised her as an enemy, Langsdorff successfully confused British Naval Intelligence by changing the name of his ship, sometimes to *Deutschland*, sometimes to *Admiral Scheer*.

long range, an error of judgment which allowed the *Doric Star*'s radio officer ample time to ensure that a distress message was picked up by the ss *Port Chalmers* for relaying to Freetown before Captain W. Stubbs surrendered to *force majeure*. But the *Doric Star* had no sooner been boarded than Langsdorff had to order her to be scuttled before she could be fully searched, in order to respond to a distress message from his own aircraft which had run out of fuel and made an enforced descent. The plane was found and recovered shortly before nightfall.

Having stirred the hornet's nest in this area, Langsdorff set his ship on a course for the Plate. At sunrise next day he had the luck to find another victim, the 7983-ton steamer *Tairoa* homeward bound from Melbourne with a cargo of meat, wool and lead. Dawn allowed the *Graf Spee* to close within two miles before Captain W. B. S. Starr realised her identity. Even so his radio operator had time to clear a distress message, coincidentally received and relayed to Freetown by the ss *Port Chalmers*, before his instruments were wrecked by gunfire. An hour later, after her crew had been transferred, the *Tairoa* was sunk.

Three days more and Langsdorff met his supply ship for the last time. The *Graf Spee* was topped up with fuel and the bulk of the crews of the *Doric Star* and *Tairoa* ferried to her. As an exception to Langsdorff's rule, two captains, Brown of the *Huntsman* and Starr of the *Tairoa*, were accommodated in the *Altmark* so that they could look after their Lascar crews.

From this rendezvous in the middle of the South Atlantic, Langsdorff continued his westward voyage. Almost at once, towards evening on December 7, he sighted the ss *Streonshalh*, of 3895 tons homeward bound with more than 5000 tons of wheat loaded at Montevideo. In the hope that the approaching warship would prove to be a British cruiser, Captain J. J. Robinson, delayed transmitting a distress message until it was too late. The sinking of the *Streonshalh*, after her crew had been transferred to the *Graf Spee*, brought the pocket-battleship's bag to nine defenceless ships of a tonnage little more than 50000 tons (*summarised in Appendix 16*), from which—and this epitomises Langsdorff's chivalry—not one life was lost.

Although Robinson had done his best to get rid of his secret documents by throwing them overboard in weighted bags, the German boarding party managed to salvage one, from which Langsdorff learned that British shipping leaving the Plate steered for a focal area some 300 miles to the east, before turning north-north-east to clear Pernambuco for Freetown, *en route* for the UK. He now knew more than the best position to find his next victim; Berlin had warned him, with fair accuracy, of the considerable British and French forces which were searching for him. But all their capital ships and aircraft carriers in the South Atlantic were reported to be in the Freetown area, and destined for Cape Town. Four British cruisers off the South American seaboard between Rio de Janeiro and the Falklands were too weak a force to deter Langsdorff from continuing towards his next operational area, which he changed from Santos Bay, to the south of Rio, to the Plate when he learned that a convoy of four ships was expected to sail from Montevideo on December 10.

On the morning of the 11th the *Graf Spee*'s seaplane made its usual dawn reconnaissance flight, to sight nothing. This was also its last flight: by the time it was hoisted inboard it had cracked an engine cylinder, and the *Graf Spee* carried no more spares.

Two days later Langsdorff's ship reached the area where he expected to find rich prey and turned on to a south-easterly course. But as the southern summer day dawned clear and cloudless on December 13, he saw more than he bargained for. He had assumed that the British cruisers were operating singly, either on patrol or escorting groups of merchant ships. Instead, 'at about 0552 there appeared off the starboard bow at first two and then four thin masts. . . . The ship went to action stations and by 0600 . . . sufficient of the superstructure of the righthand ship could be seen to identify her as HMS *Exeter*. . . . At 0610 the two smaller vessels [after first being mistaken for destroyers] were identified as HMS *Ajax* and HMNZS *Achilles*.'

CHAPTER TWO

The Hunt for the Admiral Graf Spee

Hunting Groups Organised

Nothing is more indicative of the effect of the operations of the *Graf Spee* and *Deutschland* than the extensive countermeasures which the British and French Navies were impelled to take against these two lone raiders. The damage which they did to Allied seaborne trade is to be measured not by their small 'bag', only twelve vessels totalling less than 60000 tons in two and a half months, but by the number of warships which had to be employed to hunt them down and to give direct protection to Atlantic convoys. These numbered as many as four battleships, four battle-cruisers, six aircraft carriers and more than 20 cruisers.

The British Admiralty, headed since September 4 by the redoubtable Winston Churchill as First Lord, had some reason to suspect that *one* pocket-battleship *or* an 8in cruiser was at large soon after the outbreak of war. But because neither the *Admiral Graf Spee* nor the *Deutschland* commenced operations until September 26, no specific intelligence to this effect became available until October 1. On that day the crew of Langsdorff's first victim, the ss *Clement*, was landed in South America, and from them Whitehall learned that she had been sunk by a vessel incorrectly identified as the *Admiral Scheer*.

Four days later, after consultation with Admiral Darlan who headed the French Ministry of Marine, orders went out to form eight hunting groups each fast enough to catch a pocket-battleship or 'Hipper' class cruiser, and with the offensive power to sink her. The 8in cruisers *Berwick* and *York* comprised Force F covering the coast of North America. The 8in cruisers *Cumberland* and *Exeter* and the 6in cruisers *Ajax* and *Achilles* constituted Force G off the south-east coast of South America. The 8in cruisers *Sussex* and *Shropshire* were sailed from Alexandria through the Suez Canal to form Force H covering the area off the Cape of Good Hope. The aircraft carrier *Eagle* and the 8in cruisers *Cornwall* and *Dorsetshire* were detached from the China Station to be Force I in the Indian Ocean. Force K, comprising the battle-cruiser *Renown* and the aircraft carrier *Ark Royal*, left the Home Fleet to cover the Pernambuco region. The French provided Force L, the battle-cruiser *Dunkerque*, the aircraft carrier *Béarn* and three 6in cruisers, to cover the eastern part of the North Atlantic. Force M, consisting of the French 8in cruisers *Dupleix* and *Foch*, operated out of Dakar. And to form Force N the French battle-cruiser *Strasbourg* went from Brest to the West Indies to join the aircraft carrier *Hermes* from the British Home Fleet.* Other counter-measures included sending the battleships *Resolution* and *Revenge* and the 6in cruisers *Emerald* and *Enterprise* from the Home Fleet to Halifax to escort homeward bound North Atlantic convoys.

The Search Begins

These dispositions had no sooner been ordered than the *Stonegate*'s distress message was received. But since this did not identify her assailant, and since it was geographically possible for her to have been the victim of the vessel which had sunk the *Clement*, the Admiralty dared to hope that only one pocket-battleship was at large in the Atlantic. And it was nearly three weeks before they received any further news, apart from having their suspicions aroused when ships which had failed to transmit a distress signal became overdue at their destinations. Then, on October 21, the crew of the ss *Lorenz W. Hansen* was landed by another vessel in the Orkneys, to report that they had been attacked by the *Deutschland*. This was confirmed next day by the arrival of the ss *City of Flint* at Murmansk with a prize crew from this pocket-battleship onboard. And on the same day Freetown received the ss *Trevanion*'s distress message. But no sooner had the Admiralty deduced from this that one raider was operating in the North Atlantic and another in the South, than the *Rawalpindi*'s report of being attacked by the *Deutschland* in the Faeroes–Iceland passage, suggested that this ship was bound for home.

The release of the masters of the *Clement* and *Stonegate* did something to clear this fog: they confirmed that two pocket-battleships, identified as the *Deutschland* and *Admiral Scheer*, *had* been operating in the Atlantic. But whether they were still doing so was another matter.

* For a summary of these hunting groups and of others formed later, see Appendix 5. For particulars of the principal British warships involved, see Appendix 7.

Nonetheless, the force already sent to Halifax for convoy escort duty was now augmented by the battle-cruiser *Repulse* and the aircraft carrier *Furious* from the Home Fleet, and by the battleship *Warspite* from the Mediterranean; the battleship *Malaya* and the aircraft carrier *Glorious* were passed through the Suez Canal into the Indian Ocean; and Forces M and N were replaced by Forces X and Y, the former comprised of the *Hermes*, *Dupleix* and *Foch*, the latter of the *Strasbourg*, *Neptune* and a French 6in cruiser, both to cover the Dakar–Pernambuco area.

Since the *Malaya* and *Glorious* were in the Aden area and Force I patrolled the waters near Ceylon, there was no Allied warship in the vicinity of the Mozambique Channel when the *Graf Spee* sank the tanker *Africa Shell*. But the searches of the various hunting groups in the Atlantic during this month of November were not entirely fruitless. The German ss *Uhenfels* was intercepted by the *Ark Royal*, the ss *Adolph Woermann* by the *Neptune*, both in the South Atlantic, and the ss *Emmy Friederich*, whose cargo included carbonic acid intended for the *Graf Spee*'s refrigerating plant needed to keep her magazines at a safe temperature in the tropics, by the *Caradoc* in the Gulf of Mexico.

Force G Finds the Enemy

Three of the hunting groups, Forces G, H and K, had been placed under the orders of the C-in-C South Atlantic, and it is with these that this book is chiefly concerned—and especially with Force G, Commodore Henry Harwood's South American Division whose movements were handicapped by International Law which allowed his ships to fuel only once every three months in a neutral Argentinian, Brazilian or Uruguyan port.

The arrival of the 6in cruiser *Achilles*, Captain W. E. Parry, to join this force at the end of October, allowed the 51-year-old 'Bobby' Harwood to transfer his broad pendant from the 8in cruiser *Exeter*, Captain F. S. ('Hooky') Bell, to the 6in cruiser *Ajax*, Captain C. H. L. Woodhouse, so that the former might go to the Falklands. She was joined there by the 8in cruiser *Cumberland* at the beginning of December to guard against the possibility that the enemy might decide to attack Port Stanley to avenge Admiral Graf von Spee's defeat by Admiral Sturdee on December 8, 1914. Meantime, the *Ajax* watched the River Plate area whilst the *Achilles* patrolled off Rio de Janeiro.

The German 11in gunned pocket-battleship *Admiral Graf Spee* at Spithead for the Coronation Review in 1937 [IWM

Captain Hans Langsdorff, commander of the *Admiral Graf Spee* in 1939 [BMF

Grand Admiral Erich Raeder, who was head of the Reichmarine in 1939 [IWM

Top: Another prewar picture of the *Admiral Graf Spee* [BZWS

Above: An Arado 196 seaplane, as carried by the *Admiral Graf Spee* in 1939 [IWM

The *Admiral Graf Spee*; a stern view [BZWS

The 11in guns of the *Admiral Graf Spee* [BZWS

Top: The German 8in gunned cruiser *Admiral Hipper* [IWM

Above: The German 11in gunned battle-cruiser *Gneisenau*, sister-ship of the *Scharnhorst* [IWM

Right: The British First Sea Lord in 1939, Admiral Sir Dudley Pound [IWM

Below: Commander-in-Chief of the British Home Fleet in 1939, Admiral Sir Charles Forbes [IWM

Below right: The British Commander-in-Chief South Atlantic in 1939, Admiral Sir D'Oyly Lyon [IWM

The *Admiral Graf Spee* at sea
[BZWS

The *Graf Spee*'s first victim, the Booth Line freighter *Clement*
[RTHPL

Left: Captain W. Stubbs, Master of the Blue Star liner *Doric Star* when she was sunk by the *Graf Spee* [RTHPL

Above: Captain J. M. Edwards, Master of the ss *Trevanion*, another of the *Graf Spee*'s victims [RTHPL

Left: Commodore Henry Harwood, in command of the British squadron at the Battle of the Plate: a photograph taken after he had been promoted to admiral [IWM

Below: Commodore Harwood's flagship, the 6in gunned cruiser *Ajax*, with her crew mustered on deck to see the destruction of the *Graf Spee* [IWM

Opposite, top: The French battle-cruiser *Dunkerque*: the *Strasbourg* was a sister ship [IWM

Opposite, centre: The British 15in gunned battle-cruiser *Renown* [IWM

Opposite, foot: The British aircraft-carrier *Ark Royal* [IWM

Above: The *Ajax* in action: a photograph taken off the Normandy Beaches in 1944 by which time she had been fitted with tripod masts to carry air-warning radar [IWM

Opposite, top: Captain C. H. L. Woodhouse, who was in command of the *Ajax* at the Battle of the Plate [IWM

Opposite, foot: A Fairey Seafox aircraft, as carried by HMS *Ajax* [IWM

The New Zealand Navy's 6in gunned cruiser *Achilles*: a post-1939 photograph taken after the removal of 'X' turret and the addition of tripod masts to carry air warning radar [IWM

Captain W. E. Parry, who was in command of HMNZS *Achilles* at the Battle of the Plate [IWM

The British 8in gunned cruiser *Exeter* hoisting out one of her Walrus aircraft [IWM

Catapulting a Vickers Supermarine Walrus amphibian aircraft [IWM

Captain F. S. Bell, who was in command of the *Exeter* at the Battle of the Plate [RTHPL

The British 8in gunned cruiser *Cumberland*: a post-1939 photograph taken after fitting radar [IWM

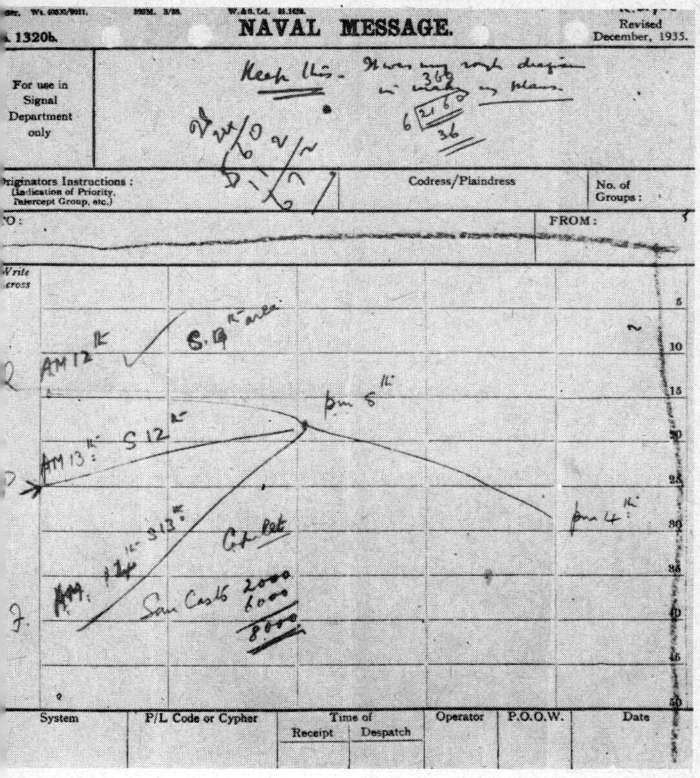
1320b.

NAVAL MESSAGE.

Revised December, 1935.

For use in Signal Department only

Keep this – It was my rough diagram in making my plans.

Originators Instructions: (Indication of Priority, Intercept Group, etc.)

Codress/Plaindress

No. of Groups:

TO:

FROM:

Write across

AM 12th

pm 8th

AM 13th

S 12th

pm 4th

2000
6000
8000

System | P/L Code or Cypher | Time of Receipt | Despatch | Operator | P.O.O.W. | Date

Commodore Harwood's sketch, on a sheet of signal pad, showing his estimate of the likely movements of the *Admiral Graf Spee* in South American waters in December 1939 [IWM

Right: HMNZS *Achilles* pursuing the *Graf Spee* on December 13, 1939. Note the blistered 6in guns of 'A' and 'B' turrets [IWM

Below: The 6in director control tower of the *Achilles*, damaged in the battle [IWM

On receiving the *Trevanion*'s raider report Admiral Lyon ordered Forces H and K to her area, and subsequently to patrol to the south of the Cape of Good Hope. But these countermeasures were taken too late to be effective. These four powerful ships achieved no more than the sinking of the German merchantman *Watussi*, by the *Renown* on December 2. On that date Lyon received the *Doric Star*'s raider report and immediately redisposed his ships. Force H was ordered to cover the trade route from the Cape to the latitude of St Helena while Force K swept northwest from the Cape to Freetown. Again these moves were not made in vain: on December 9 the *Shropshire* caught the ss *Adolph Leonhardt*, though she failed to prevent her being scuttled by her crew.

Four days earlier, on the western side of the South Atlantic, the *Ajax* and *Cumberland* had likewise been baulked of their prey, the ss *Ussukama*. Harwood had then to send the *Cumberland* back to Port Stanley for a self-refit. Although the *Doric Star* had been sunk nearly 3000 miles from the focal area which his force was covering, the Commodore was convinced that sooner or later the rich traffic off the South American coast would tempt the enemy. Having calculated that the *Doric Star*'s assailant could reach the Rio focal area by December 12, the Plate by the 13th, and the Falkland Islands by the 14th, he opted for the second of these as the most vital one to be defended, and decided to concentrate his available cruisers there. On December 3 he ordered HMS *Exeter* to leave Port Stanley on the 9th, and HMNZS *Achilles* to close his flagship, HMS *Ajax*. These three ships thus met at a rendezvous 150 miles to the east of the estuary of the Plate at 0700 on the 12th.

Next morning they were steaming in single line ahead on a mean course of 060 degrees at the slow speed of 14 knots in order to conserve fuel. Although the *Exeter* carried two Walrus amphibian aircraft and the *Ajax* a Seafox seaplane for spotter-reconnaissance duties, none was launched for a dawn patrol. According to the *Exeter*'s observer:

'I'm afraid we were not very air conscious in those days.'

But Harwood had to conserve his aircrafts' engine hours; the *Ajax*'s second aircraft was already unserviceable. Moreover, he could not suppose his calculations to be so accurate, or his decision to guard the Plate area so sure, that he would find the enemy there as soon as that morning. The point is, however, only important in that it was to deprive him of all but one plane to carry out spotting duties during the battle.

For soon after dawn his insight into Langsdorff's mind was proved to be as sure as Nelson's into Brueys'. When smoke was sighted at 0614* on December 13 bearing some degrees, the *Exeter* was ordered to close and investigate. Two minutes later Bell signalled:

'I think it is a pocket-battleship.'

* According to Harwood's Despatch on the battle; but there is considerable evidence that the smoke was sighted some ten minutes earlier, *i.e.* very soon after the *Graf Spee* identified her largest opponent as HMS *Exeter*, *vide* p. 35.

CHAPTER THREE

The Battle

The Action Begins

Langsdorff's memorandum, written near the end of November, has been quoted in Chapter 1. Specifically, 'the necessity for avoiding action damage [being] no longer so pressing, if the *Graf Spee* was to close the range her powerful armament would at least so damage an opponent as to eliminate him as a shadower'. *An* opponent. But now, on December 13, Langsdorff was faced with *three*. What then should his tactics be? With a speed disadvantage of some seven knots the odds were against eluding the enemy without a fight. According to Winston Churchill:

> 'His right course would have been to turn away immediately so as to keep his assailants as long as possible under the superior range and weight of his 11in guns, to which the British could not at first have replied.'*

But could Langsdorff have crippled all three enemy vessels before the *Graf Spee* had expended her ammunition? The battle-cruisers *Invincible* and *Inflexible* fired 80 per cent of their outfits of 12in shell (600 rounds) to sink the fleeing armoured cruisers *Gneisenau* and *Scharnhorst* off the Falklands in December 1914. The quicker Langsdorff closed the range the sooner the *Graf Spee*'s 11in shells could be expected to score damaging hits on cruisers which had no effective protection against them, and which could reply with nothing larger than 8in. So, at 0600,** eight minutes after first sighting the enemy and as soon as his ship was cleared for action, Langsdorff altered course towards and increased to full speed, which because of a foul bottom was only 24 knots. Fifteen minutes later, when the range was inside 20000 yards, he turned to port to bring both 11in turrets to

* *The Second World War*, Vol. I.

** All times in this Chapter are Zone+2.

bear on his strongest opponent, HMS *Exeter*. Three minutes more and the *Graf Spee* opened fire.

Harwood had for long reflected on the tactics which he would employ. Though faced with a heavily armed and armoured vessel, he had more compensating advantages than a higher speed. He had a force which could be divided and engage from different bearings, and a larger number of guns which could maintain a much higher rate of fire than the enemy's bigger weapons. Moreover, unlike the unfortunate Troubridge in his pursuit of the *Goeben* in August 1914, his orders left him in no doubt that he was required to put an end to the *Graf Spee*'s career as a commerce raider. So, at noon on December 12, he had signalled:

> 'My policy with three cruisers . . . versus one pocket-battleship. Attack at once. By day act as two units. First Division [*Ajax* and *Achilles*] and *Exeter* diverged to permit flank marking [of gunfire]. First Division will concentrate gunfire . . .'

With these clear instructions Bell needed no further orders when, at 0616, he decided that the smoke bearing 320 degrees probably came from a pocket-battleship. He was already diverging from the *Ajax* and *Achilles*: he had only to ring down for full speed, swing his ship on to a course of 280 degrees to bring the *Exeter*'s three turrets to bear and, at 0620, two minutes after the *Graf Spee*, open fire. Harwood had meantime ordered the *Ajax* and *Achilles* to increase speed and turn to 340 degrees to close the range. And at 0621, when it was down to 19400 yards, the First Division likewise opened fire. Two minutes later this was being controlled by W/T from the flagship (*i.e.* in concentration firing), with the *Achilles* conforming with the *Ajax*'s movements three to four cables astern, but with Parry manoeuvring her as necessary to clear Woodhouse's line of fire.

The First Phase: 0614–0640

The *Graf Spee*'s gunfire was all too accurate. Her third salvo straddled the *Exeter*, one shell bursting short amidships and its splinters killing the starboard torpedo tubes' crew. They also damaged her two Walrus aircraft, which her catapult's crew were trying to launch, so that both had to be jettisoned. This left only the *Ajax*'s Seafox to carry out spotting duties, but, though successfully launched at 0637, some fifteen minutes elapsed before W/T communication was established for this purpose (a delay explained in *Appendix 12*).

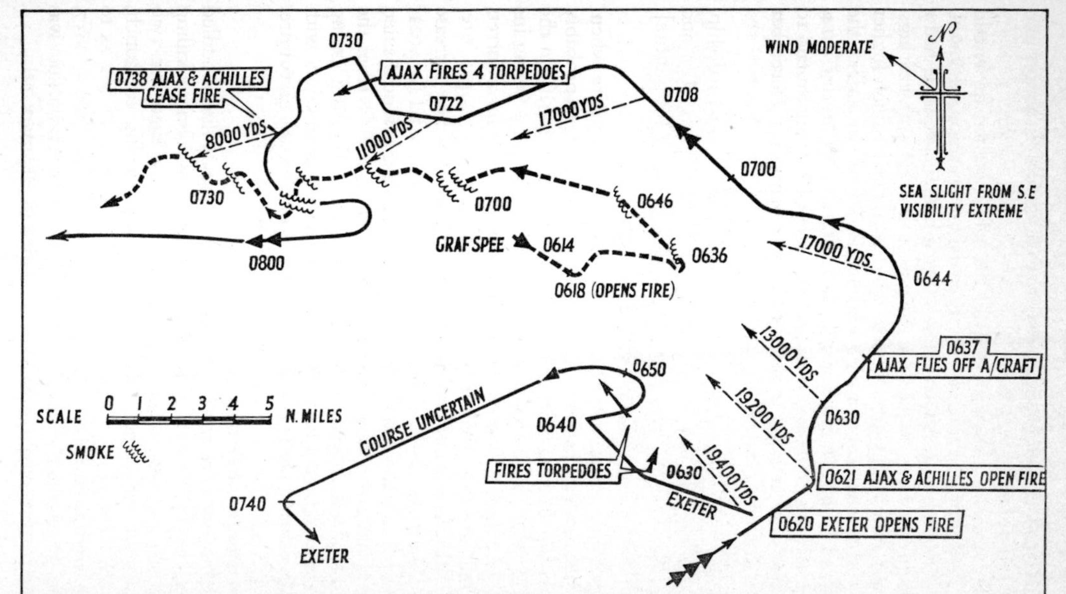

Diagram 2. The Battle of the River Plate, 0614–0740

For a very different reason the *Exeter* was never able to flank mark the First Division's gunfire. After firing only eight salvoes, of which the third was a straddle, and surviving a shell which went through the deck and ship's side abaft 'B' turret without exploding, she received a direct hit on the front of 'B' turret. This not only put it out of action but swept the bridge with splinters that killed all who were there, except for her captain and two other officers, and wrecked the wheelhouse communications. Bell, though suffering a facial wound, went aft and continued fighting his ship from the secondary conning position, with the handicap of having to pass all orders to the after steering position through a hurriedly improvised chain of messengers. And by the time this had been organised the *Exeter* had suffered two more damaging hits forward.

The *Graf Spee* was not, however, escaping punishment. One of the *Exeter*'s shells had struck her control tower, and by 0630 Langsdorff was so worried by the gunfire of the *Ajax* and *Achilles* that, although they were now within range of his secondary armament, and so under fire by the *Graf Spee*'s 5·9in and 4·1in guns, he ordered his 11in to shift target. (He did not, be it noted, divide his main armament because effective shooting was not to be expected of only three heavy guns.) As a result, these two British cruisers were in turn straddled but, by weaving, were able to avoid being hit by anything more damaging than splinters from bursts short.

In the brief respite which this gave to the *Exeter*, her torpedo officer fired her starboard tubes in local control at 0632. To avoid this threat and, coincidentally, a salvo from the *Exeter*'s port tubes six minutes later, as well as the *Ajax*'s and *Achilles*' 6in rapid salvoes at a range that was by now down to 13000 yards, Langsdorff altered course as much as 150 degrees away to port under cover of a smoke screen. He also re-directed his main armament on to its original target, when the *Exeter*, after achieving her second hit on the *Graf Spee*, was struck by two more 11in shells, one of which put 'A' turret out of action, and the other started a fierce fire amidships. This severed her fire control circuits and put all her gyro repeaters out of action, so that, to Bell's other difficulties, was added that of having to con his ship by nothing better than a boat's portable compass.

The Second Phase: 0640–0740

Although the action was far from being over, by 0637, the time that Langsdorff altered course 120 degrees away from the enemy, only twenty minutes after opening fire, he was a beaten man. Confronted by three lightly protected cruisers whose commander had determined to *attack* instead of, as Langsdorff expected, being content to shadow, he lacked the resolution to adhere to his intended swift and devastating close range battle. He could have continued the *Graf Spee*'s swing to port right round to the southwest and concentrated on giving the *coup de grâce* to the *Exeter*, which was now able to engage only with her after turret in local control. But though the 6in shells of the *Ajax* and *Achilles* failed to penetrate the *Graf Spee*'s armour, he feared the damage which they were doing to her superstructure, and the casualties which they were inflicting on the exposed crews of her secondary armament guns. He changed his tactics to engaging these two small cruisers at long range, now some 17000 yards.

This allowed the *Exeter* to continue the fight—as a potential threat rather than to any other effect—despite an 11in hit which flooded several compartments forward and caused a seven degree list. Almost miraculously, she suffered no damage to her engine or boiler rooms so that she retained her speed. Bell was, therefore, able to keep the *Graf Spee* under fire, albeit without scoring any hits, until 0729 when the electricity supply to 'Y' turret's machinery failed. Not until then did a very gallant captain, 61 of whose officers and men had been killed, and 23 wounded, break off the action. And not for another twenty minutes (0750) did the much damaged *Exeter*'s log record:

'Enemy disappeared to westward pursued by *Ajax* and *Achilles*.'

The battle had turned into a chase. At 0710 Harwood tired of engaging his enemy at long range. Accepting the loss of 'A' arcs,* he turned more directly in pursuit to the westward and increased to full speed. To thwart this move, Langsdorff made a drastic alteration to port under cover of smoke; then, at 0720, he turned back to starboard far enough to open the *Graf Spee*'s 'A' arcs on the First Division. The range having dropped to 11000 yards, the *Ajax* was quickly straddled by three 11in salvoes. Harwood promptly turned his ships to open their 'A' arcs again, when they scored hits on their opponent which started a fire amidships. Five minutes later the *Graf Spee* had her revenge: an 11in shell struck the *Ajax* aft, putting both

* These are the arcs in which a ship can bring all its main armament guns to bear.

'X' and 'Y' turrets out of action, damage far more serious than anything achieved by the hits scored by the enemy's secondary armament.

Almost simultaneously, the *Ajax* turned to starboard and fired four torpedoes at a range of 9000 yards. Langsdorff swung his ship 130 degrees to port to avoid this salvo, then turned back to fire his own ship's starboard tubes. The tracks of these torpedoes were seen by the *Ajax*'s aircraft in time to warn Harwood to turn the First Division away to avoid them.

These turns apart, the action continued with the *Graf Spee* heading west, every now and again under a protective smoke screen, with the two British cruisers in pursuit, until 0738. With the range then down to 8000 yards, Harwood learned that the *Ajax* had fired 80 per cent of her ammunition. Since he could assume that the *Achilles* had expended a similar quantity, and since the *Graf Spee*'s shooting remained disturbingly accurate, one salvo bringing down the *Ajax*'s main topmast and all her W/T aerials, he decided to break off the day action and close in again after dark. Accordingly, at 0740, after a brisk engagement that had lasted for an hour and twenty minutes, the *Ajax* and *Achilles* turned away to the east under cover of smoke—a decision to which Harwood held even though he subsequently established that it was only the *Ajax*'s 'A' turret which had fired so much ammunition.

The Pursuit: 0740–2350

Langsdorff, who had suffered two splinter wounds (in the shoulder and in the arm), made no attempt to round on his adversaries. He kept the *Graf Spee* on a course almost due west for the estuary of the River Plate at 24 knots, whilst the *Ajax* and *Achilles* followed her at the safe distance of 15 miles, a task made easy by the size of the enemy's control tower. The pocket-battleship's captain had decided to seek refuge in the neutral port of Montevideo.

Although the *Graf Spee* had put the *Exeter* out of action—Langsdorff believed that she was in a sinking condition and would never reach harbour—she had expended 60 per cent of her ammunition. And since the two British 6in cruisers retained their speed advantage, he had no confidence in his chances of being able to cripple them with what remained. Even if he did so, the *Graf Spee* would be left with too little with which to face an encounter with units of the Home Fleet when she tried to return to Germany.

Then there were the *Graf Spee*'s casualties (none of them, fortunately, among her 62 British prisoners—including the whole of the ss *Streonshalh*'s crew whom Langsdorff had had no chance to transfer to the *Altmark*). In addition to 36 dead, she had six seriously wounded, who would have to be landed for hospital treatment before he attempted the run for home, as well as 53 with lesser injuries.

More important, however, was the damage which three 8in and 17 6in shells had inflicted on the pocket-battleship (*see Appendix 14*). Although only one had pierced her armoured deck, and none had affected her immediate battleworthiness, she had a large hole in her bows above water which would have to be repaired before she faced winter weather in the North Atlantic. And much of her superstructure, including her galleys and bakery, and the plant for purifying the fuel and lubricating oil for her engines, had been wrecked: here, too, repairs beyond the ship's resources were needed before she attempted the long voyage home.

But these three factors are not in themselves enough to explain Langsdorff's decision to take the *Graf Spee* into Montevideo. His apologists contend that his judgment was impaired by his wounds, but there can be no doubt that he was impelled to do so by the skill and tenacity of his puny opponents. They had shown that the British Navy had lost neither the fighting ability nor the courage with which it had so often gained a victory against odds in the past—or, like Sir Richard Grenville in the *Revenge*, established an immortal tradition. Who then shall criticise him beyond saying that a British officer in his predicament—many thousands of miles from a friendly port, pursued by an enemy which he could not shake off, and which could be expected to summon more powerful vessels to the scene—would have chosen a fight to the death. And that would have been a more glorious end for the *Graf Spee* than the one for which she was destined.

Around 0800 Harwood ordered the *Ajax*'s aircraft to locate the *Exeter* and ascertain why she did not answer W/T calls transmitted by the *Achilles*. (The *Ajax* was still rigging jury aerials.) She was soon located 'obviously hard hit', ablaze amidships and 'in no condition to fight another action'. She did not, however, need immediate assistance. The *Ajax* then recovered her aircraft.

At 0916 Harwood ordered the *Cumberland* to leave the Falklands at full speed. Despite the handicap of having boilers opened up to repair brickwork, she sailed from Port Stanley as soon as 1000,

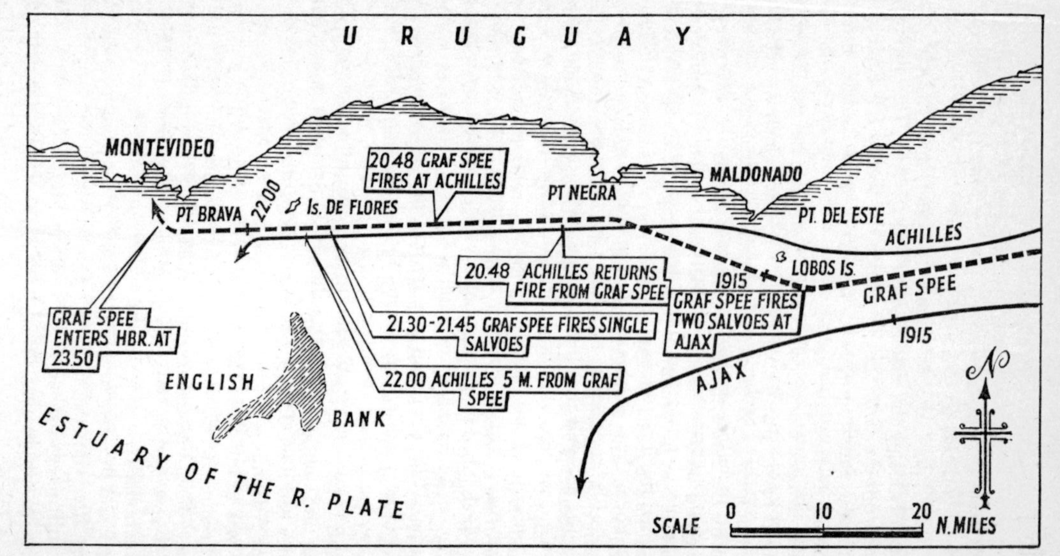

Diagram 3. The *Admiral Graf Spee*'s approach to Montevideo

because Fallowfield had raised steam on his own initiative when, around 0630, his ship began intercepting messages indicating that Force G was in action. Even so, it was a long haul to the mouth of the Plate, 36 hours at 30 knots.

At 1005 Parry overestimated the enemy's speed, and made the mistake of closing the *Achilles* in to 23000 yards. This drew two 11in salvoes from the *Graf Spee*, of which the second fell close alongside. Parry immediately turned away under cover of smoke, and resumed shadowing from a safer range.

An hour later Harwood received a signal from the *Exeter*. Having managed to rig jury aerials, Bell was able to report her condition. Only one gun in 'Y' turret remained in action, and she was so far down by the bows that her speed was limited to 18 knots. To this there could be only one reply. Bell was ordered to proceed to Port Stanley as best he could without straining the *Exeter*'s bulkheads.

The *Ajax* and *Achilles*, whose combined casualties totalled, almost miraculously, only 11 killed and 5 injured, continued to shadow the *Graf Spee* throughout the rest of a day that was disturbed only by minor incidents. At 1543 Parry sighted a vessel which appeared to be a 'Hipper' class 8in cruiser. Some twenty minutes elapsed before his and Harwood's anxiety at this unexpected development was relieved by the stranger's true identity—the new ss *Delane*, of the Lamport & Holt Line, whose streamlined funnel was similar to the *Hipper*'s. And at 1915, more than an hour after first sighting the Uruguayan coast, the *Graf Spee* suddenly altered course and fired two salvoes at the *Ajax* at a range of 26000 yards, causing her to turn away under smoke.

Long before this Langsdorff had signalled a brief action report to Berlin and announced his intention to enter Montevideo, to which Raeder had replied, 'Agreed'. Harwood had also signalled the British Naval Attaché in Buenos Aires, Captain H. McCall, that the *Graf Spee* was heading for the Plate as early as 1347. But not until 1900 was he sure that the enemy intended to enter this wide deep water estuary. Then he ordered the *Achilles*, which had suffered no damage except splinters, to follow her if she went west of Lobos Is., the International Law of hot pursuit overriding the sanctity of territorial waters, and the *Ajax* to turn south in case she doubled back that way.

Just after sunset at 2048, off Punta Negra, the *Graf Spee*, which was still more than 50 miles from her intended haven, fired three salvoes to ensure that the *Achilles* kept her distance, to which she replied with five. As darkness fell Parry had to close in order to maintain touch, and he was not deterred from doing so by three final salvoes, fired by the *Graf Spee* between 2130 and 2145. But he had no need to reduce the range below 10000 yards: having held her westward course to pass to the north of English Bank, the pocket-battleship was by this time clearly silhouetted against the lights of Montevideo. And in that neutral city's Roads Parry saw her drop anchor shortly before midnight. A few minutes later an officer entered the compartment in which the *Graf Spee*'s British prisoners had had the nerve-wracking experience of being confined throughout the battle. 'Gentlemen,' he announced, 'the Captain has told me to say that you will be freed tomorrow.'

Harwood could not touch the *Graf Spee* now; nor could he safely remain within the mouth of the Plate, even if he had been prepared to ignore Uruguay's territorial waters. One of his ships had two of her turrets out of action, and the best part of twenty-four hours must elapse before the *Cumberland*, with her 8in guns and full outfit of ammunition, could join him. Yet he had no idea for how long the *Graf Spee* would stay in Montevideo; he had to be prepared for her to leave at any time. And if she came out in the morning he had to avoid the serious disadvantage of being caught against the dawn light. The best he could do was to order the First Division to withdraw and to patrol to seaward of the Plate, the *Achilles* in a sector from the Uruguayan coast to a line drawn 120 degrees from English Bank, and the *Ajax* to the south of this line—and await the enemy's next move.

Meantime, there could be no doubt as to who had won the battle of the Plate. Harwood's splendid achievement was recognised by his immediate promotion to rear-admiral and the award of the KCB, and Bell's, Parry's and Woodhouse's by the CB (*see Appendix 15*).

CHAPTER FOUR

The End of the Admiral Graf Spee

Reinforcements for Force G

There followed intense activity in Montevideo, and widespread movements by British naval units across the South Atlantic. For the President of Uruguay and his Cabinet, for British and German diplomats, for Whitehall and the Wilhelmstrasse, and for the C-in-C South Atlantic in his Freetown headquarters, as well as for the principal actors, Harwood and Langsdorff, in a tense drama which radio news commentators now carried to a world-wide audience, the chief problem was the same: for how long should, or would, the *Graf Spee* remain in Montevideo Roads?

As soon as he received news of the battle on December 13, Admiral Lyon signalled the 8in cruiser *Dorsetshire* of Force I to leave Cape Town at high speed for the Plate. Thirty-six hours later the Admiralty ordered her sister-ship, the *Shropshire*, to follow, and placed both under Harwood's orders. On the same date the battle-cruiser *Renown* and the aircraft carrier *Ark Royal*, of Force K, were directed to Rio de Janeiro for fuel. There these two ships were joined on the 17th by the 6in cruiser *Neptune* from Force Y; and thence all three were to hurry south at full speed. In addition, to guard against the *Graf Spee* escaping round the Cape of Good Hope into the Indian Ocean, the aircraft carrier *Eagle*, the 8in cruiser *Cornwall* and the 6in cruiser *Gloucester*, were ordered to Durban, and placed at the disposal of Admiral Lyon.

An overwhelming concentration—one battle-cruiser, two aircraft carriers and eight cruisers—were thus directed towards the danger point, the estuary of the River Plate. But such were the distances that many of these ships had to steam—2500 miles in the case of the *Ark Royal* and *Renown*, more than 3500 for the *Dorsetshire* and *Shropshire*—that there was no possibility of achieving it before December 19. And in the intervening days much could—and did—happen.

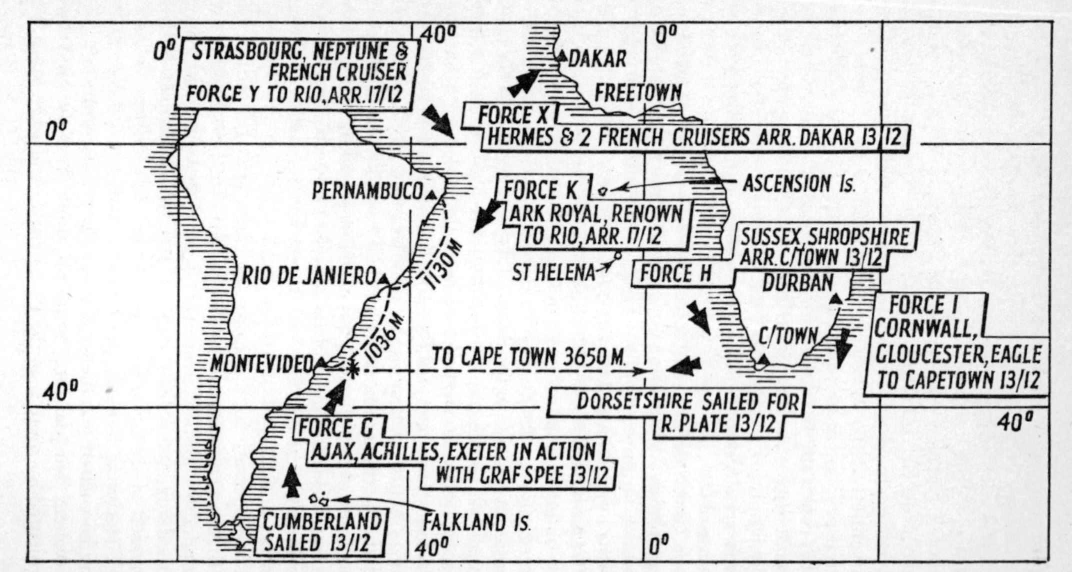

Diagram 4. Hunting Groups in the South Atlantic, December 13, 1939

Diplomacy in Montevideo, December 14–16

For General Alfredo Baldomir, President of Uruguay, and his Ministers for Foreign Affairs, Dr Alberto Guani, and of National Defence, General Alfredo Campos, who wished to preserve their country's friendly relations with Britain but could not ignore an active pro-Nazi minority, the problem was one of interpretation and enforcement of International Law. According to the Hague Convention of 1907 a belligerent warship could prolong its stay in a neutral port for more than 24 hours only *if* it had suffered damage. In that case it might 'carry out such repairs as are absolutely necessary to render [it] seaworthy, [but] may not add in any manner whatever to [its] fighting force. The . . . neutral Power shall decide what repairs are necessary, and these must be carried out with the least possible delay'.

The *Graf Spee* had not, therefore, been at anchor in Montevideo Roads for very long before Guani and Campos were subjected to two opposing arguments. The German Minister, Otto Langmann, advised by his Naval Attaché, Captain Dietrich Niebuhr, pressed for the *Graf Spee* to be allowed to stay for as long as 15 days. Langsdorff gave as his reason the need to make his ship seaworthy; but he wanted also to make her battleworthy. Conversely, the British Minister, Mr Eugen Millington-Drake, advised by his Naval Attaché, McCall, argued that since the *Graf Spee* had steamed at high speed for some 300 miles from the scene of the battle into Montevideo, she was clearly seaworthy and should not be allowed to stay for more than 24 hours. In response to these arguments, Guani and Campos told the German Minister that they would instruct their technical experts to inspect the *Graf Spee*'s damage, whilst Millington-Drake was reminded that the cruiser *Glasgow* had been allowed to dock in Rio for the best part of a week to effect repairs after the battle of Coronel in 1914.

The inspection took place on the 14th, after Langsdorff had freed his British prisoners, and landed his dead for burial and his seriously wounded for hospital treatment. But before Guani and Campos had finished reviewing their experts' report, the British Minister was reminded of Talleyrand's advice to his diplomatists: *'n'ayez trop de zèle'*. Harwood signalled early on the 15th to the effect that the last thing he wanted was the *Graf Spee*'s early departure: on the contrary he wanted her detained until his puny battle-scarred force was augmented by more than the *Cumberland*. And there was a legitimate way of doing this: the Hague Convention included a *caveat*: 'a belligerent warship may not leave a neutral port less than 24 hours after the departure of a merchant ship flying the flag of her adversary —to give the latter a fair chance to evade capture'.

So, whilst McCall hastened to arrange for the ss *Ashworth* to leave Montevideo that evening, Millington-Drake had to ask Campos to ensure that the pocket-battleship did not sail before 1800 on the 16th. This embarrassing *volte-face* was, however, superfluous: Campos replied that his Government had already decided to grant the *Graf Spee* an extension of 72 hours to effect repairs, chiefly to the large hole in her bows, such as were within her own resources. Montevideo's only shipyard would not help.

But for Langsdorff this was far from being a satisfactory solution. According to reports deliberately spread by British sources, the Plate was *already* blockaded by the *Renown* and *Ark Royal*. Indeed, his gunnery officer believed that he could see them on the horizon from the *Graf Spee*'s control tower. When he signalled this intelligence to Berlin, together with the news that he was required to sail not later than the evening of the 17th, or face internment for both ship and crew in Uruguay for the duration of the war, Langsdorff added that there was 'no prospect of breaking out into the open sea and getting through to Germany. If I can fight my way through to Buenos Aires [the Argentine being more friendly to Germany than Uruguay] with ammunition still remaining I shall endeavour to do so'. But as this 'might result in destruction . . . without possibility of causing damage to the enemy, request instructions whether to scuttle the ship . . . or to submit to internment'. On this Langmann commented:

> 'I regard internment as the worst possible solution. It would be preferable in view of [the *Graf Spee*'s] shortage of ammunition, to blow her up in the shallow waters of the Plate and to have the crew interned.'

After consulting Hitler, Raeder who rightly believed in leaving the ultimate decision to the man on the spot, answered:

> 'Attempt by all means to extend the time in neutral waters. . . . Approved [to fight your way through to Buenos Aires if possible]. No internment in Uruguay. Attempt effective destruction if ship scuttled.'

And the German Foreign Office replied in the same sense to Langmann, adding (an unconscious tribute to Millington-Drake and McCall) that he was to 'counter with the greatest possible energy the influence of the British'. So Langmann and Niebuhr again pressed for the *Graf Spee*'s stay to be extended—but to no effect. Guani's and Campos's determination to respect International Law, coupled with Millington-Drake's and McCall's pressure on them to do so, proved too strong. Early on the 17th Langsdorff accepted his fate: since the Führer had forbidden internment—his fanatical pride would not accept such an ignoble defeat—the *Graf Spee* would leave Montevideo that evening.

Day of Reckoning: December 17

Harwood's first concern had been to ensure that the *Graf Spee*, which could leave the estuary of the Plate by three widely diverse routes, did not do so unobserved. To this end he had split his force, ordering the *Ajax*, *Achilles* and *Cumberland* to patrol in separate seaward sectors. But by the 16th he judged, not least from the reports being broadcast by American radio commentators who had flown to Montevideo, that he could rely on receiving immediate news of any movement by the enemy, and of the course which Langsdorff chose to steer. This allowed him to concentrate his force in the southern part of the estuary ready to engage the *Graf Spee* as soon as she left international territorial waters, using the same 'divided tactics' as on the 13th, with the *Cumberland* taking the *Exeter*'s place as his Second Division. 'My object destruction', he signalled his captains; even so he estimated that the *Graf Spee* had a 70 per cent chance of escaping him.

But this was far from being Langsdorff's assessment. Because he supposed the *Renown* and *Ark Royal* to be waiting for him, he believed that he had no real chance of breaking-out. And he would not send his officers and men to almost certain death: that might be the British tradition, but it was not the German. Since the Uruguayan Government insisted that the *Graf Spee* should sail by 2000 on December 17, he was left with only one alternative.

Early that morning he gave the necessary orders. First, the ship's secret documents and equipment, especially for fire control, were destroyed. Next, large scuttling charges, including torpedo warheads with time fuses, were placed in several of the ship's large compartments, and in her main magazines. Finally, 700 of her crew

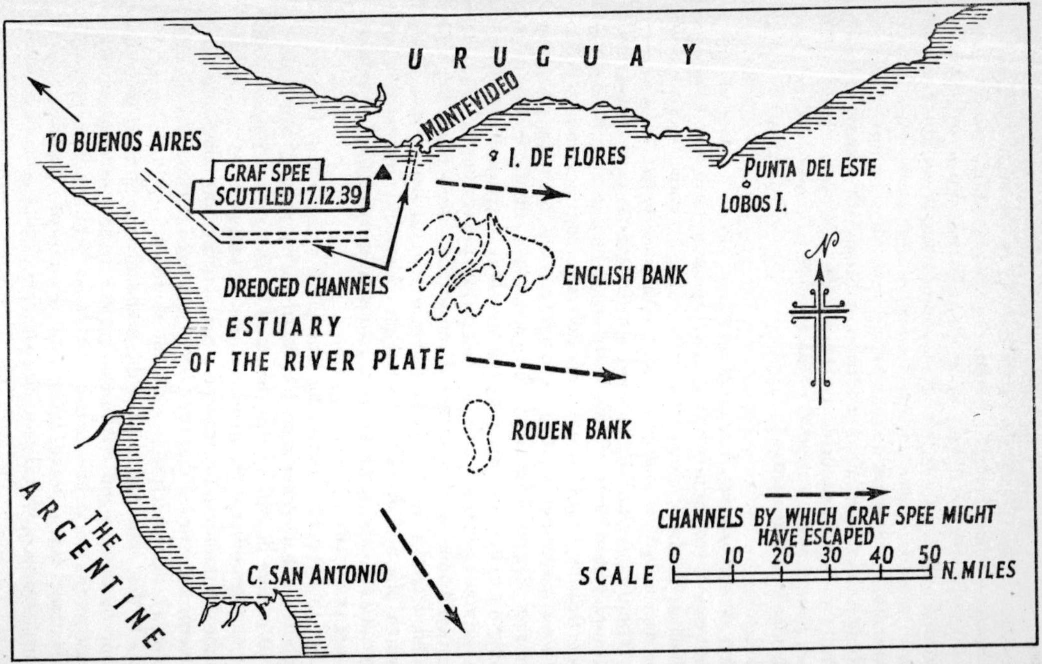

Diagram [illegible] The *Admiral Graf Spee*'s possible escape routes

were transferred to the ss *Tacoma*, a German tanker of 8268 tons, Captain Hans Konow, which was lying in the Roads. Those who remained made the final preparations for their ship's last voyage.

Shortly after 1800 Langsdorff gave the order to weigh. Watched from the shore by a crowd of many thousands, the pocket-battleship, with the Nazi ensign flying from fore and main, moved out of Montevideo heading southeast. She was followed by the *Tacoma*, about a mile astern. Four miles out, at the end of the dredged channel and a mile outside territorial waters, the *Graf Spee* altered course, not to seaward but sharply to the west. Then she stopped and again dropped anchor. The time fuses were set, and Langsdorff and his skeleton crew left the ship in their own boats. Twenty minutes later, at 2000 and shortly after sunset, the *Graf Spee* was rent from end to end by heavy explosions. She sank almost immediately in water so shallow that her control tower, turrets and superstructure could still be seen, a mass of tangled wreckage shrouded in smoke and fire.

The *Tacoma* took Langsdorff and his skeleton crew onboard, but Konow's attempt to head for the friendly neutrality of Buenos Aires was frustrated by an Uruguayan warship. The latter persuaded the *Tacoma* to return to Montevideo (where she was later interned for having violated Uruguayan neutrality by assisting with a hostile act); but only after the *Graf Spee*'s crew had transferred to waiting Argentine tugs which the Germans had arranged to be there to cover just such an eventuality.

Harwood had headed his three cruisers nearer to Montevideo around the time the *Graf Spee* was expected to leave, and ordered the *Ajax* to catapult her plane. It was, wrote *Achilles*' gunnery officer,*

> 'a glorious evening with a vivid sunset over the Argentine coast. We were closed up and loaded, ready for whatever might come. . . . We received the news that she had sailed. . . . We could hear the Yankee broadcasters [describing us as] "the suicide squadron with their little popguns. . . ." And then, enormous moment, *Ajax*'s machine [radioed], "*Graf Spee* has just blown herself up" . . . We continued to close and gradually the burning hulk came up on the horizon. The Germans had made a very thorough job of it. She burned fiercely. . . . Towards midnight we approached within a few miles of the pyre . . . then turned away.'

* Lieutenant R. E. Washbourn in a letter to a friend.

That night Harwood and his officers and men relaxed, secure in the certainty that the battle which they had fought with such skill and gallantry 300 miles from the mouth of the River Plate four days before, had ended in such a victory as was always Nelson's ambition, the total destruction of the enemy.

Captain Langsdorff's Death

Langsdorff expected that he and his crew would receive a warm welcome when they landed in Buenos Aires, and that they would be treated as shipwrecked seamen. Instead, he was attacked by the press as a coward, and as a traitor to the tradition of the sea, because he had not gone down with his ship; and the Argentine Government decided that he and his crew should be interned for the duration of hostilities. Such unexpected treatment finally unbalanced a captain who had borne the heavy responsibility of three months' lone cruising in enemy infested waters, who had suffered the shock of defeat by smaller vessels, and had since been brought near to exhaustion by his unsuccessful negotiations to prolong the *Graf Spee*'s stay in Montevideo.

That evening, after saying farewell to his officers and men, Langsdorff retired to his room to write three letters, to his wife, to his parents, and to the German Ambassador, Baron von Thormann. According to the last of these:

> 'After a long inward struggle I reached the grave decision to scuttle the . . . *Graf Spee* . . . to prevent her falling into the hands of the enemy. . . . This decision was the only one I could take after I had taken my ship into the trap of Montevideo. With the ammunition remaining, any attempt to break out to open and deep water was bound to fail. . . . It was clear that this decision might be misinterpreted . . . by persons ignorant of my motives. . . . Therefore I decided . . . to bear the consequence involved. . . . A captain with a sense of honour cannot separate his own fate from that of his ship. . . . After today's decision by the Argentine Government, I can do no more for my ship's company. . . . Now I can only prove by my death that the fighting Services of the Third Reich are ready to die for the honour of their flag. I alone bear the responsibility for scuttling the . . . *Admiral Graf Spee*. . . . I shall meet my fate with firm faith in the cause and the future of the nation and of my Führer.'

This letter finished, Langsdorff unfolded a German naval ensign and drew his revolver. Next morning one of his officers found him lying dead on the ensign. The whole of the *Graf Spee*'s crew attended his funeral that afternoon. So did Captain Pottinger of the ss *Ashlea*, representing all his victims, as a last tribute to a chivalrous foe, who had died honourably but, as subsequent years were to prove, for a vain cause.

In the same letter Langsdorff wrote:

> 'Neither will I be able to take any further active part in the present conflict of my country.'

This was true of the great majority of the *Graf Spee*'s crew who were dispersed in a number of internment camps until the Argentine joined the Allies in March 1945, when they became prisoners of war. But there were exceptions: 16 officers escaped between January and April 1940, a further group of 17 in August of that year, and a few more in 1942. There was also a small handful of ratings who likewise managed to return to Germany by diverse routes, notably across the Pacific and by way of Japan and the USSR, to rejoin the war. Indeed, as captain of *U-162*, one officer sank 86000 tons of Allied merchant shipping, half as much again as the total sunk by the *Graf Spee*. But the great majority 'enjoyed Argentinian hospitality' until February 1946, when six officers and 894 ratings were repatriated onboard the British liner *Highland Monarch*, escorted—a nice touch of irony this—by HMS *Ajax*. 168 ratings chose to remain in the Argentine where many more rejoined them later. Today some 500 of the *Graf Spee*'s crew are settled there. But their ship is no longer to be seen: after December 1939 the wreck sank slowly into the mud until, by 1948, only the control tower remained above water.

'The Navy's Here!'

The lot of the 299 British officers and men held prisoner onboard the *Altmark* was not a happy one. Dau ignored Langsdorff's order to land them in some neutral port: to show his ship in this way must endanger her safe return to Germany. He went south instead, to an area where there was no other shipping, to wait until Berlin advised him that it would be safe to run for home. And because his own crew was too small, despite the addition of an armed guard from the *Graf Spee*, to provide many sentries, he had to keep his prisoners in confined quarters under rigid discipline and, for lack of provisions for such a considerable number of captives, feed them on a restricted diet.

The *Altmark* stayed in the deep South Atlantic until January 22, 1940. Then, five weeks after the battle, she headed north to cross the Equator on the 31st. Eleven days later she passed through the Denmark Strait. Three days more and, still unreported, she reached the apparent safety of neutral Norway's territorial waters. Though she was stopped twice by Norwegian torpedoboats who asked if she had anyone onboard from the belligerent powers, both accepted Dau's assurance that he had none. But the Norwegian admiral at Bergen was far from satisfied: on his orders the captain of the torpedoboat *Kjell* sent an officer on board the *Altmark* when she entered his area on February 15. But, not surprisingly, Dau refused to allow his ship to be searched; and because the *Altmark* was a naval auxiliary rather than a merchant ship, the *Kjell*'s captain decided that he could do no more than follow her south to see that she committed no obvious breach of Norwegian neutrality.

Fortunately for Dau's captives, the British Navy was determined to spare them the rigours of a German prison camp. When, on the evening of the 15th, Admiral Forbes learned that the *Altmark* was off Bergen, he signalled the 6in cruiser *Arethusa*, Captain Q. D. Graham, which with the *Cossack* and four other destroyers was retiring from a sweep into the Skagerrak:

'*Altmark* your objective. Act accordingly.'

She was spotted next day, steaming south down the Leads, the passage inside Norway's off-shore islands, first by a patrolling plane of RAF Coastal Command, and then by a keen-eyed look-out on the *Arethusa*'s bridge. Since the Admiralty had already signalled that the *Altmark* might be intercepted inside territorial waters, Graham promptly ordered his destroyers to go after her. But those which arrived first were prevented from boarding by the Norwegian torpedoboats *Kjell* and *Skarv* steaming close alongside, whilst Dau turned his ship into the greater safety of Josing Fiord.

She was there when, as darkness fell, Captain Philip Vian came up in the *Cossack*. Informing the senior Norwegian officer that there were British prisoners onboard, he demanded the right to search for them. When a determined Norwegian replied that his orders were to resist, any such action, and trained his torpedo tubes on the *Cossack*,

Vian sought the Admiralty's instructions. They came three hours later from Churchill and Pound in no uncertain terms:

> 'Unless Norwegian torpedoboat undertakes to convoy *Altmark* to Bergen with a joint Anglo-Norwegian guard onboard and a joint escort, you should board *Altmark*, liberate the prisoners and take possession of ship. . . . Suggest to Norwegian captain that honour is served by submitting to superior force.'

For a man of Vian's character these words, and the need to be well clear of waters where he might be subjected to air attack after dawn next day, were enough. The Norwegian warships were soon persuaded to withdraw from the scene, leaving the *Cossack* to go alone through the narrow entrance into Josing Fiord, where the *Altmark* was seen in the light of a full moon, her great bulk black against the snow-clad mountains. Risking the possibility that she might open fire, Vian headed the *Cossack* alongside. Dau tried turning a blinding searchlight on the British vessel's bridge; then went full speed astern in an attempt to ram the intruder. But to no avail: the possibility of a damaging collision was ended when the *Altmark* grounded by the stern. This not only allowed the *Cossack* to go alongside, but her first lieutenant, Bradwell Turner, and two other officers to lead 30 armed seamen onboard.

The armed guard from the *Graf Spee* offered resistance: six Germans were killed and six wounded before they escaped ashore. Now free to investigate the *Altmark*'s holds, Turner ordered the hatches to be broken open. 'Any British down there?' he called. 'Yes,' came a tremendous yell, 'we're all British.' 'Come on up then,' said Turner, adding his now immortal words:

> 'The Navy's here!'

The *Altmark* had to be left in Josing Fiord until Dau could free her stern. Then, under cover of darkness, he completed his return to Germany, but without the satisfaction for which he had hoped. His British prisoners, 13 officers and 286 seamen, had already reached the safety of Leith on February 17, to receive the fervent welcome which was their due, just two months after the *Graf Spee*'s destruction.

Verdict

Early in January 1940 the *Ajax* paid a triumphant visit to Montevideo, whilst the *Achilles* was as warmly received in Buenos Aires. Both ships then sailed for home, the *Ajax* to England for repairs to her after turrets, the *Achilles* to New Zealand. On Churchill's insistence the much damaged *Exeter* was also brought back with a strong escort.

The *Achilles* reached Auckland on February 22 where Parry and his officers and men were as loudly cheered as Woodhouse and Bell with their crews when, on that same day, after being inspected by the King on Horse Guards Parade, they marched through the streets of London to a banquet in Guildhall.

Churchill gave this verdict when he boarded the *Exeter* on her return to Plymouth and addressed her ship's company:

> 'In this sombre dark winter, when . . . we have had to watch the agony of Poland and now of Finland, the brilliant action of the Plate, in which you played a memorable part, came like a flash of light and colour on the scene, carrying with it an encouragement to . . . ourselves and to our Allies. . . . Here at Plymouth . . . we are able to congratulate you upon the fortune which enabled you to fight an action in the old style . . . which will long be told in song and story . . . carrying us back to the days of Drake and Raleigh, to the great sea days of the olden times. . . . [You can] say to them, "We, your descendants . . . have not forgotten the lessons you taught. . . ." You have all lost good comrades and shipmates . . . but you . . . have come back with the firm knowledge of having . . . faithfully accomplished a worthy cause, with your honours gathered and with your duty done'.

And the Navy's poet, Admiral Ronald Hopwood, was inspired to pen this tribute:

> *There's a wreck at the mouth of a river, that once was*
> *the pride of her land,*
> *That men, passing by, may consider—observing the works*
> *of their hand,*
> *Aforetime so proud and so mighty—what succour can*
> *Science afford*
> *When faced by the Captains Courageous, whose hearts*
> *are the works of the Lord.*

The *Admiral Graf Spee* in Montevideo Roads after the battle, showing her burnt-out Arado aircraft and damage to the port side of her hull below the after pair of 5.9in guns [IWM

The *Admiral Graf Spee* shortly after being destroyed by her own crew outside Montevideo Roads [IWM

The *Admiral Graf Spee*'s fore turret, bridge and control tower, after being blown up on December 17, 1939 [IWM

The *Admiral Graf Spee* burning after her destruction. Note the radar aerial on the foreside of the control tower [IWM

Top: HMS *Ajax* visits Montevideo after the battle (*A picture sent by radio.*) [IWM

Above: Commodore Harwood being greeted by the British Minister, Mr Eugen Millington-Drake at Montevideo in December 1939 (*A picture sent by radio.*) [IWM

Panzerschiff Admiral Graf Spee

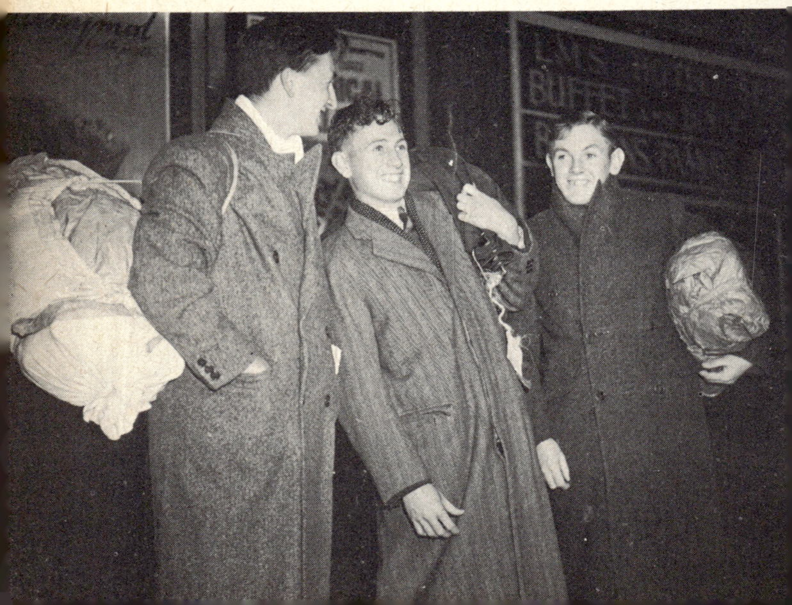

BUFFET

Opposite, top: Captain P. Dove, Master of the ss *Africa Shell*, returns to England in January 1940 with one of the *Graf Spee*'s cap ribbons [RTPHL

Opposite, foot: Three British prisoners of the *Graf Spee* on their arrival in England in January 1940 [RTPHL

Above: The British destroyer *Cossack* [IWM

Right: Captain Philip Vian on the bridge of the *Cossack* [IWM

ALTMARK
ALTMARK

Opposite, top: The German supply ship, *Altmark*, aground in Josing Fiord [UPI

Opposite, foot: Another view of the *Altmark* in Josing Fiord [IWM

Above: The damaged cruiser *Exeter* returns to Devonport in February 1940 (*Painted by Charles Cundall, RA.*)

Britain's First Lord of the Admiralty, Mr Winston Churchill, cheered by Captain F. S. Bell and the officers of HMS *Exeter* after he had addressed her ship's company at Devonport in February 1940 [RTPHL

HM King George VI inspects and decorates the ships' companies of HMS *Ajax* and *Exeter* on Horseguards Parade on February 23, 1940 (*Painted by Sir Muirhead Bone.*) [IWM

PART TWO

Statistical Data

APPENDIX ONE

Chronological Summary

1939	
August 3:	*Altmark* sails from Wilhelmshaven and steams down Channel.
August 21:	*Admiral Graf Spee* sails from Wilhelmshaven.
August 24:	*Graf Spee* passes between Faeroes and Iceland. *Deutschland* and *Westerwald* sail from Wilhelmshaven.
August 28:	*Graf Spee* fuels from *Altmark* northwest of Azores. *Deutschland* passes through Denmark Strait.
August 30:	*Deutschland* and *Westerwald* reach waiting area south of Greenland.
September 3:	**Britain and France declare war on Germany.**
September 5:	President Roosevelt declares Pan-American Neutrality Zone.
September 11:	*Graf Spee*'s aircraft sights *Cumberland.*
September 13:	*Graf Spee* reaches waiting area in South Atlantic and fuels from *Altmark.*
September 20:	*Graf Spee* refuels from *Altmark.*
September 26:	*Graf Spee* and *Deutschland* ordered to commence operations.
September 30:	*Graf Spee* sinks SS *Clement* off Pernambuco.
October 1:	Admiralty deduces that *one* raider is in the Atlantic.
October 5:	Anglo-French hunting groups formed in Atlantic and Indian Ocean. Powerful escorts provided for North Atlantic convoys. *Graf Spee* captures SS *Newton Beech* south of Freetown. *Deutschland* sinks SS *Stonegate* east of Bermuda.
October 7:	*Graf Spee* sinks SS *Ashlea.*
October 8:	*Deutschland* captures SS *City of Flint.*
October 8–10:	Sortie by *Gneisenau* and *Köln.*
October 9:	Aircraft from HMS *Ark Royal* sights *Altmark* west of Cape Verde Islands, but believes her to be US tanker. SS *Newtown Beech* sunk.

October 10: *Graf Spee* captures ss *Huntsman.*

October 14: *Deutschland* sinks ss *Lorenz W. Hansen* east of Newfoundland.

October 15: *Graf Spee* returns to waiting area and refuels from *Altmark.*

October 17: ss *Huntsman* sunk.

October 21: Crew of ss *Lorenz W. Hansen* landed in Orkneys.

October 22: *Graf Spee* sinks ss *Trevanion* on Cape–UK trade route. ss *City of Flint* reaches Murmansk. *Caradoc* intercepts ss *Emmy Friederich.*

October 29: *Graf Spee* returns to waiting area and refuels from *Altmark.*

November 1: *Deutschland* recalled to Germany.

November 3: *Graf Spee* enters Indian Ocean.

November 5: *Ark Royal* intercepts ss *Uhenfels.*

November 8: *Deutschland* returns through Denmark Straits. Admiralty learns that *two* raiders *were* operating in the Atlantic. British forces in North Atlantic and Indian Ocean strengthened.

November 15: *Graf Spee* sinks ss *Africa Shell* in Mozambique Channel. *Deutschland* arrives Gotenhaven.

November 16: *Graf Spee* approaches ss *Mapia.*

November 20: *Graf Spee* returns to South Atlantic.

November 21: *Gneisenau* and *Scharnhorst* leave Wilhelmshaven.

November 22: HMS *Neptune* intercepts ss *Adolph Woermann.*

November 23: *Gneisenau* and *Scharnhorst* sink *Rawalpindi* in Iceland–Faeroes passage.

November 27: *Graf Spee* refuels from *Altmark* in waiting area. *Gneisenau* and *Scharnhorst* return to Wilhelmshaven.

End of November: Force G: *Cumberland* and *Exeter* at the Falklands; *Ajax* off the Plate: *Achilles* off Rio de Janeiro. Forces H and K patrolling south of Cape of Good Hope.

December 2: *Graf Spee* sinks ss *Doric Star* on Cape–UK trade route. Forces G, H and K redisposed to counter her. *Renown* sinks ss *Watussi.*

December 3: *Graf Spee* sinks ss *Tairoa.*

December 5: *Ajax* and *Cumberland* intercept ss *Ussukama.*

December 6: *Graf Spee* refuels from *Altmark.*

December 7: *Graf Spee* sinks ss *Streonshalh.*

December 9: *Shropshire* intercepts ss *Adolf Leonhardt*. *Cumberland* arrives Falkland Islands. Commodore Harwood orders *Achilles* and *Exeter* to join *Ajax*.

December 12: Force G (*Ajax*, *Achilles* and *Exeter*) concentrates 150 miles east of Plate estuary.

December 13: Force G sights *Graf Spee*. Battle of the River Plate. *Exeter* damaged, heads for Falkland Islands. *Cumberland* leaves Falkland Islands for the Plate. *Ajax* and *Achilles* follow *Graf Spee* into Montevideo Roads, then remain on patrol off Plate estuary.

December 14: German Minister asks Uruguay Government to allow *Graf Spee* to remain in Montevideo for 15 days to effect repairs. *Dorsetshire* ordered from Cape Town to the Plate. *Cumberland* joins Force G.

December 15: *Shropshire* ordered from Cape Town to the Plate. *Renown*, *Ark Royal* and *Neptune* ordered to Rio de Janerio for fuel. *Eagle*, *Cornwall* and *Gloucester* ordered to the Cape. ss *Ashworth* sailed from Montevideo to delay *Graf Spee* sailing until 16th. Uruguay decides to allow *Graf Spee* to remain in Montevideo until 1800 on December 17.

December 16: Berlin instructs Langsdorff to scuttle *Graf Spee*.

December 17: *Renown*, *Ark Royal* and *Neptune* arrive Rio and sail for the Plate. *Graf Spee* blown up in Plate estuary, with help of ss *Tacoma*.

December 18: *Graf Spee*'s crew interned in Buenos Aires. *Tacoma* subsequently interned in Montevideo.

December 19: Langsdorff commits suicide.

1940

January: *Ajax* returns to England.

January 22: *Altmark* begins run for home.

February 11: *Altmark* passes through Denmark Strait.

February 14: *Altmark* enters Norwegian territorial waters.

February 15: *Exeter* returns to Plymouth. *Altmark* passes Bergen.

February 16: *Altmark* seeks refuge in Josing Fiord where boarded by *Cossack* and all British prisoners released.

February 23: *Achilles* returns to New Zealand. *Ajax* and *Exeters*' companies inspected by King George VI on Horse Guards Parade, and entertained in Guildhall.

APPENDIX TWO

Distribution of British Fleet, September 1939

(Capital ships, aircraft carriers and cruisers)

Home Waters

Battleships:	7	(*Nelson, Rodney, Ramillies, Revenge, Resolution, Royal Oak, Royal Sovereign*)
Battle-cruisers:	3	(*Hood, Renown, Repulse*)
Aircraft carriers:	4	(*Ark Royal, Courageous, Furious, Hermes*)
8in cruisers:	2	(*Norfolk, Suffolk*)
6in cruisers:	19	(*Aurora, Belfast, Edinburgh, Effingham, Emerald, Enterprise, Glasgow, Newcastle, Sheffield, Southampton* and 9 of old 'C' and 'D' classes)

Mediterranean

Battleships:	3	(*Barham, Malaya, Warspite*)
Aircraft carrier:	1	(*Glorious*)
8in cruisers:	3	(*Devonshire, Shropshire, Sussex*)
6in cruisers:	3	(*Arethusa, Galatea, Penelope*)

North Atlantic

7.5in cruiser:	1	(*Hawkins*)
6in cruisers:	2	(of old 'C' class)

America and West Indies

8in cruisers:	2	(*Berwick, York*)
6in cruisers:	2	(*Orion, Perth*)

South Atlantic

8in cruisers:	2	(*Cumberland, Exeter*)
6in cruisers:	6	(*Ajax, Neptune* and four old 'D' class)

East Indies

6in cruisers:	3	(*Gloucester, Liverpool, Manchester*)

China

Aircraft carrier:	1	(*Eagle*)
8in cruisers:	3	(*Cornwall, Dorsetshire, Kent*)
6in cruiser:	1	(*Birmingham*)

Australia

8in cruisers:	2	(*Australia, Canberra*)
6in cruisers:	3	(*Adelaide, Hobart, Sydney*)

New Zealand

6in cruisers:	2	(*Achilles, Leander*)

In Home Dockyards for modernisation

Battleships:	2	(*Queen Elizabeth, Valiant*)
8in cruiser:	1	(*London*)
7.5in cruiser:	1	(*Frobisher*)

APPENDIX THREE

Distribution of French Fleet, September 1939

(Capital ships, aircraft carriers and cruisers)

North Atlantic
Battle-cruisers: 2 (*Dunkerque, Strasbourg*)
Aircraft carrier: 1 (*Béarn*)
Cruisers: 3

Mediterranean
Battleships: 3
Aircraft carriers: 10
Cruiser: 1
Large destroyers: (*i.e.* light cruisers): 28

Far East
Cruisers: 2

APPENDIX FOUR

Distribution of German Fleet, September 1939

(Capital ships and cruisers)

Western Area (Wilhelmshaven)

Battle-cruisers:	2	(*Scharnhorst, Gneisenau*)
Pocket-battleship:	1	(*Admiral Scheer*)
8in cruiser:	1	(*Admiral Hipper*)
5·9in cruisers:	5	(*Emden, Köln, Königsberg, Liepzig, Nürnberg*)

Eastern Area (Kiel)

Pre-dreadnought battleships:	2	(*Schlesien, Schleswig-Holstein*)

Ocean Warfare

Pocket-battleships:	2	(*Admiral Graf Spee, Deutschland*)

APPENDIX FIVE

Composition of British and French Hunting Groups

Name of Force	*Composition*	*Type of ship*	*Area of operations*	*Detached from*
F	*Berwick*	8in cruiser	North America	—
	York	8in cruiser	and West Indies	—
G	*Exeter*	8in cruiser	Southeast coast	—
	Cumberland	8in cruiser	of South	—
	Achilles	6in cruiser	America	New Zealand
	Ajax	6in cruiser		—
H	*Shropshire*	8in cruiser	Cape of Good	Mediter-
	Sussex	8in cruiser	Hope	ranean
I	*Eagle*	Aircraft carrier	Ceylon	China
	Cornwall	8in cruiser		China
	Dorsetshire	8in cruiser		China
K	*Renown*	Battle-cruiser	Pernambuco	Home Fleet
	Ark Royal	Aircraft carrier		Home Fleet

L	*Dunkerque*	Battle-cruiser	Brest	—
	Béarn	Aircraft carrier		—
	Gloire	6in cruiser		—
	Montcalm	6in cruiser		—
	Georges Leygues	6in cruiser		—
M	*Dupleix*	8in cruiser	Dakar	Mediter-ranean
	Foch	8in cruiser		
N	*Strasbourg*	Battle-cruiser	West Indies	Brest
	Hermes	Aircraft carrier		Plymouth
X	*Hermes*	Aircraft carrier	Dakar–Pernambuco	Force N
	Dupleix	8in cruiser		Force M
	Foch	8in cruiser		Force M
Y	*Strasbourg*	Battle-cruiser	Dakar–Pernambuco	Force N
	Neptune	6in cruiser		—
	1 French	6in cruiser		—

APPENDIX SIX

Summary of Merchant Ships Sunk, etc.

(a) **By the Graf Spee** (see also Appendix 16)

Clement	Sunk September 30.
Newtown Beech	Captured October 5. Sunk October 9.
Ashlea	Sunk October 7.
Huntsman	Captured October 10. Sunk October 17.
Trevanion	Sunk October 22.
Africa Shell	Sunk November 15.
Doric Star	Sunk December 2.
Tairoa	Sunk December 3.
Streonshalh	Sunk December 7.

(b) **By the Deutschland**

Stonegate	Sunk October 5.
City of Flint (US)	Captured October 8. Arrived Murmansk in prize October 22.
Lorenz W. Hansen (Nor.)	Sunk October 14.

(c) **By British Warships**

Emmy Friederich	Intercepted by *Caradoc* October 22 and scuttled by own crew.
Uhenfels	Intercepted by *Ark Royal* November 5 and scuttled by own crew.
Adolph Woermann	Intercepted by *Neptune* November 22 and scuttled by own crew.
Watussi	Sunk by *Renown* December 2.
Ussukama	Intercepted by *Ajax* and *Cumberland* December 5 and scuttled by own crew.
Adolf Leonhardt	Intercepted by *Shropshire* December 9 and scuttled by own crew.

APPENDIX SEVEN

British Ships Data

Ships at the Battle of the River Plate

Achilles (Cruiser)

Displacement:	7030 tons standard.
Dimensions:	530 (pp), 554½ (oa) × 55¼ × 16ft.
Machinery:	4 Admiralty three drum boilers; 4 shafts; Parsons geared turbines, 72000 SHP = 32½ knots; 1800 tons oil.
Protection:	Main belt 2–4in, deck 2in, turrets 1in.
Armament:	8–6in/50 cal (4 × 2), 4–4in/40 cal (4 × 1) HA; 8–21in (2 × 4) TT. 1 catapult.*
Complement:	577.
Builder:	Cammell Laird, Birkenhead.
Laid down:	11.6.31.
Launched:	1.9.32.
Completed:	10.10.33.
Cost:	£1545780.
Fate:	To RIN (renamed *Delhi*) 1948.

Ajax (Cruiser)

Displacement:	6985 tons standard.
Dimensions:	530 (pp), 554½ (oa) × 55¼ × 16ft.
Machinery:	4 Admiralty three drum boilers; 4 shafts; Parsons geared turbines, 72000 SHP = 32½ knots; 1800 tons oil.
Protection:	Main belt 2–4in, deck 2in, turrets 1in.
Armament:	8–6in/50 cal (4 × 2), 8–4in/40 cal (4 × 2) HA; 8–21in (2 × 4) TT. 2 Fairey Seafox aircraft** and 1 catapult.
Complement:	593.
Builder:	Vickers-Armstrong, Barrow.
Laid down:	7.2.33.
Launched:	1.3.34.

* Her Fairey Seafox aircraft was accidentally lost before she left New Zealand to join Force G.

** On December 13, 1939 one of these was no longer operational.

Completed: 3.6.35.
Cost: £1491417.
Fate: Scrapped 1949.

Exeter (Cruiser)
Displacement: 8390 tons standard.
Dimensions: 540 (pp), 575 (oa) × 58 × 17ft.
Machinery: 8 Admiralty three drum boilers; 4 shafts; Parsons geared turbines, 80000 SHP = 32 knots; 1900 tons oil; radius 10000 miles at 14 knots.
Protection: Main belt 2–3in, deck 2in, turrets $1\frac{1}{2}$–2in.
Armament: 6–8in/50 cal (3 × 2), 4–4in/40 cal (4 × 1) HA; 6–21in (2 × 3) TT; 2 Vickers Supermarine Walrus aircraft and 1 catapult.
Complement: 616.
Builder: HM Dockyard, Devonport.
Laid down: 8.28.
Launched: 18.7.29.
Completed: 5.31.
Cost: £1839345.
Fate: Sunk in Java Sea, 1.3.42.

Note

The 1922 Washington Naval Treaty, signed by Great Britain, the USA, France, Italy and Japan, limited the size of cruisers to 10000 tons with guns not exceeding 8·1in calibre, but imposed no limit on their number. Since the USA intended to build cruisers of this size, Britain did likewise with the 'County' class, armed with eight 8in guns, of which the *Cumberland* was among the first. When financial stringency made clear the impracticability of maintaining Britain's cruiser strength at 70 with vessels so large, the smaller 'Cathedral' class of 8400 tons armed with six 8in guns was begun with the *York* and *Exeter*. Only these two ships and thirteen 'Counties' had been laid down or completed when, for further reasons of economy, the Admiralty reverted to its old policy of building cruisers armed with 6in guns, a decision reinforced by the London Naval Treaty signed in 1930, which limited the British Commonwealth to a total of fifteen 8in cruisers. The *Ajax* and *Achilles* were two of the eight ships of the 'Leander' class, of approximately 7000 tons, armed with eight 6in guns, which were then built.

Other Ships involved (brief details only)

Type	*Name*	*Completed*	*Displacement (Standard)* tons	*Main Armament* in	*Speed* knots	*Notes*
Battle-cruiser	*Renown*	1916	32000	6–15	29	Modernised 1936–39
Aircraft carrier	*Ark Royal*	1938	22000	16–4·5	31	60 aircraft
Do.	*Eagle*	1920	22600	9–6	24	21 aircraft
Cruiser	*Cumberland*	1928	9750	8–8	31½	
Do.	*Cornwall*	1928	9750	8–8	31½	
Do.	*Dorsetshire*	1930	9975	8–8	32	
Do.	*Gloucester*	1939	9400	12–6	32	
Do.	*Neptune*	1934	7175	8–6	32½	
Do.	*Shropshire*	1929	9830	8–8	32	
Do.	*Sussex*	1928	9830	8–8	32	
Destroyer	*Cossack*	1938	1870	8–4·7	36	

APPENDIX EIGHT

German Ships Data

Admiral Graf Spee (Pocket-battleship)

Displacement:	10000 tons nominal, 12100 tons standard, 16200 tons full load.
Dimensions:	597 (wl), 617 (oa) × 71 × 24ft.
Machinery:	Eight MAN double acting nine cylinder two-stroke diesel engines geared to two shafts; 56800 SHP= 26 knots; 2756 tons oil, radius 9000 miles at 19 knots.
Protection:	Main belt 4in, decks $1\frac{1}{4}$–$2\frac{1}{4}$in, turrets 5–$5\frac{1}{2}$in.
Armament:	6–11in/54·5 cal (2 × 3), 8–5·9in/55 cal (8 × 1), 6–4·1in/65 cal (3 × 2) HA, 8–37mm (8 × 1) HA, 8–20mm (8 × 1) HA, 8–21in (2 × 4) TT; 1 Arado 196 seaplane and 1 catapult.
Complement:	1124.
Builder:	Kriegsmarinewerft, Wilhelmshaven.
Laid down:	1.10.32.
Launched:	30.6.34.
Completed:	6.1.36.
Cost:	£3750000.
Fate:	Scuttled outside Montevideo 17.12.39.

Deutschland (Pocket-battleship)

Displacement:	10000 tons nominal, 11700 tons standard, 15900 tons full load.
Dimensions:	593 (wl), 617 (oa) × 68 × 24ft.
Machinery:	Eight MAN double-acting nine cylinder two-stroke diesel engines geared to two shafts; 56800 SHP= 26 knots; 2784 tons oil, radius 10000 miles at 19 knots.
Protection:	Main belt $3\frac{1}{4}$in, decks $1\frac{1}{2}$–3in, turrets 4–$5\frac{1}{2}$in.
Armament:	6–11in/54·5 cal (2 × 3), 8–5·9in/55cal (8 × 1), 6–3·5in/7[illegible] cal (3 × 2) HA, 8 × 37mm (4 × 2) HA, 8–20mm (8 × 1

HA; 8–21in (2×4) TT; 1 Arado 196 seaplane and 1 catapult.

Complement: 1150.
Builder: Deutsche Werke, Kiel.
Laid down: 5.2.29.
Launched: 19.5.31.
Completed: 1.4.33.
Fate: Renamed *Lützow*; scuttled Swinemünde 16.4.45, after being bombed by Allied aircraft. Salvaged by USSR. Scrapped Leningrad 1948/9.

Auxiliaries

Altmark (naval auxiliary tanker)
Tonnage: 7021 tons gross, 3535 tons net.
Dimensions: 463×68×27ft.
Machinery: Geared turbines=22 knots.
Armament: HA guns and pom-poms.
Complement: 130.
Builder: Blohm & Voss, Hamburg.
Completed: 1938.
Fate: Renamed *Uckermaris*; destroyed by petrol vapour explosion, Yokahama 30.11.42.

Tacoma (Hamburg-America Line)
Tonnage: 8268 tons gross.
Machinery: Steam turbines=15 knots.
Completed: 1930.
Complement: 62.

Notes on the evolution of the pocket-battleship

The German Admiralty began to consider how best to replace its pre-dreadnought battleships soon after signing the Treaty of Versailles. It was assumed that Germany's main enemy would be France, requiring ships adequate to counter that country's dreadnoughts in the eastern part of the North Atlantic in order to cut her supply routes and keep Germany's open. The first design, completed in 1923, for a vessel mounting four 15in guns, was rejected because it lacked armour. The alternatives of a heavy-gunned, well-protected, but slow vessel of the monitor type suitable for coast defence, or a large ocean-going cruiser were then contemplated. Neither being suitable for a war with France, fresh consideration was given to some form of battleship.

A ship mounting six 12in guns in three twin turrets was designed in 1925, but rejected for lack of secondary armament. The next two designs, for vessels with the same main armament, all mounted forward, plus four 6in guns in twin centre-line mountings, were rejected for lack of armour. Another design with six 12in mounted in two triple turrets, one forward and one aft, and with more smaller guns, lacked sufficient armour. The possibility of increasing this by reducing the 12in guns to four was then explored, followed by an investigation into the consequences of reducing the main armament to 11in guns.

The argument, speed versus armour, continued until 1927 by which time a decision had become urgent. Four designs were then considered:

Type	*Main armament*	*Main belt*	*Speed*
A	four 15in	10in	18 knots
B1	six 12in	10in	18 knots
B2	six 12in	8in	21 knots
C	six 11in	4in	26 knots

These made clear that it was impracticable to build a ship with guns comparable with a battleship's, plus the armour needed to withstand heavy shell fire, within Treaty limits. So the choice fell on Type C, a vessel with an armament heavier than any cruiser's and with a speed sufficient to elude all battleships. This would be a serious menace not only to the French Fleet but to the Fleets of other Powers. The *Deutschland* and her two sisters, classed as *Panzerschiffe* (armoured ships) for want of any precedent for such vessels, were built accordingly.

Recognising the threat which these presented, the Washington Powers made efforts to prevent their completion. In 1930 Germany was willing to abandon them provided she was accepted as a signatory to the Washington Treaty, with the right to build a battle fleet up to a tonnage ratio of 1·75, compared with Britain's and the USA's 5, and Japan's 3 and France's and Italy's 1·75. But the Powers granted no concession: moreover, at the 1930 London Naval Conference France opposed a five-year extension of the ban on battleship building so as to be able to lay down the battle-cruisers *Dunkerque* and *Strasbourg* as a counter to Germany's pocket-battleships.

To save weight and to give them a large radius of action, these incorporated two notable technological innovations. They were the first major warships to have all-electric welded hulls and to be driven by diesel engines. Even so, as completed they exceeded their declared standard displacement of 10000 tons by more than one-fifth of this figure.

APPENDIX NINE

Guns and Gunnery

Gun Data

Calibre	*Barrel length*	*Barrel weight*	*Projectile weight*	*Max range*	*Max elevation*	*Rate of fire*
British						
8in	50 cal	16·5 tons	256lb	29200yd	70°	6 rpm
6in	50 cal	8 tons	100lb	25000yd	35°	8 rpm
4in	40 cal	1·3 tons	31lb	—	HA	12 rpm
German						
11in	54·5 cal	53·2 tons	694lb	46500yd	45°	2·5 rpm
5·9in	55 cal	9·1 tons	95lb	18000yd	35°	10 rpm
4·1in	65 cal	1·5 tons	33lb	—	HA	15 rpm
37mm	83 cal	—	—	—	HA	—
20mm	65 cal	—	—	—	HA	—

Main Armaments

Ship	*Weight of a broadside*	*Possible rounds per minute*
Graf Spee	4164lb	15
Exeter	1536lb	36
Ajax	800lb	64
Achilles	800lb	64

Ammunition expended

Ship	*Calibre*	*Rounds fired*	*Hits scored*	*Rounds remaining*
Exeter	8in	193 (possibly plus)	3	approx 400
Ajax	6in	823	17 (Ajax and Achilles)	777
Achilles	6in	1241		359
Graf Spee	11in	414	8 on *Exeter*, 2 on *Ajax*	186
	5·9in	377	None	—
	4·1in	80	None	—

Rounds fired to obtain one hit

By *Exeter* 64

By *Ajax* and *Achilles* 121

By *Graf Spee* (11in) 41

Comments

For much of the action the *Graf Spee*'s 11in gunnery was considerably more accurate than the British ships' 8in and 6in, despite Langsdorff's several shifts of target which involved the need to 'find' the range afresh each time. But the *Graf Spee*'s gunnery officer underestimated the British cruisers' protection: had he used armour-piercing shell instead of HE, it is unlikely that the *Exeter* would have survived.

The 11in ammunition remaining in the *Graf Spee* amounted to 31 rounds per gun, which was only enough for a further engagement of 20–30 minutes. The *Ajax* (two turrets left) had enough 6in ammunition left for a fight of 30–40 minutes, but the *Achilles* had enough for only a 15–20 minute action.

APPENDIX TEN

Torpedoes

The torpedoes carried by the British cruisers and by the *Admiral Graf Spee* were of the then standard 21in (diameter) type developed by both navies out of those used in World War I. Length 24ft, weight 3500lb. Steam turbine driving counter-rotating propellers. Gyroscopic control of steering. Warhead filled with Torpex or a similar explosive detonated by contact pistol, weight 600lb. Typical ranges: 15000 yards at 28 knots; 10000 yards at 34 knots; 6000 yards at 46 knots. Fired at the battle of the River Plate: *Exeter* six, no hits; *Ajax* four, no hits; *Graf Spee* four, no hits. But despite this apparent failure of torpedo fire, the sharp turns away made by both sides to avoid being hit, had a considerable if temporary effect on the accuracy of their gunfire.

APPENDIX ELEVEN

Aircraft

British

Fairey 'Seafox': a very light two-seater biplane with twin floats for spotter-reconnaissance duties, designed for catapult launching. 395hp Napier-Halford 'Rapier VI' 16 cylinder 'H' type air-cooled engine. Span 40ft; length 35ft 6in; height 12ft 1in. Weight empty 3805lb; weight loaded 5420lb. Maximum speed 124mph. Range 440 miles at 90mph. Rate of climb 420ft per min. Service ceiling 11000ft.

Vickers Supermarine 'Walrus': a two-seater biplane flying boat with retractable wheeled under-carriage for spotter reconnaissance duties, designed for catapult launching. 775hp Bristol 'Pegasus VI' 9 cylinder radial air-cooled engine driving a pusher airscrew. Span 45ft 10in, length: 37ft 7in; height 15ft 3in. Weight empty 4900lb; weight loaded 7200lb. Maximum speed 135mph. Range 600 miles at 95mph. Rate of climb 1050ft per min. Service ceiling 18500ft.

German

Arado 196: a two-seater monoplane with twin floats for spotter-reconnaissance duties, designed for catapult launching. 900hp BWM 9 cylinder radial air-cooled engine. Span 40ft 10½in; length 36ft 1in; height 14ft 6in. Weight empty 6580lb; weight loaded 8200lb. Maximum speed 193mph. Range 670 miles at 158mph. Rate of climb 980ft per min. Service ceiling 23000ft.

Note

The Arado had such a high landing speed that it alighted on the sea with an excessive shock that drenched the air-cooled engine, often cracking its cylinders. So many cylinders in the *Graf Spee*'s machine had thus been damaged and replaced that by December 12, when one more cracked, no further spares were available—with the serious consequence that the machine could not be used in next day's battle.

APPENDIX TWELVE

Communications

Equipment
The British cruisers were equipped with the following W/T transmitters:

Ship	*Main long-range set*	*Secondary long-range set, and for communication with aircraft*	*Auxiliary set for communication with ships in company*	*Gunnery control set*
Achilles	48	37	43	45
Ajax	48	49	43	45
Cumberland	36	37	43	45
Exeter	36	37	43	45

Details are:

Type No	*Approx date of design*	*Frequency range*	*Rated power*
36	1926	100–550kcs 3–12mcs	5kw
37	1926	Do.	1kw
43	1926	1800–2500kcs	100watts
45	1926	2500–3500kcs	100watts
48	1934	100–550kcs 3–12mcs	5kw
49	1934	Do.	2kw

The main transmitter was aft, with an adjacent Central Receiving Room containing several receivers covering 15–550kcs and 3–15mcs. The other transmitters were in a Second Office forward (Type 37 or 49) and a Third Office (Types 43 and 45), with matching receivers. Signals received, and for transmission, were normally carried between these protected offices and the bridge, etc. by pneumatic tube; but in action the delay which this involved was not acceptable. The main, secondary and auxiliary sets were then operated from a Remote Control Office immediately below and in direct voicepipe communication with the bridge, and the gunnery set was similarly operated from the Gunnery Transmitting Station (*i.e.* fire control room).

The *Admiral Graf Spee*'s equipment was similar to that in the British ships, with the important addition of a receiver specially designed to intercept enemy transmissions.

Organisation

British ships in South American waters were handicapped by the obsolescence of the Admiralty's Falkland Islands W/T station. Having only one antiquated Marconi Type U medium frequency transmitter of 3–5kw output to which a high frequency attachment had been added, this could do no more than maintain a shore-ship broadcast on 8555kcs interrupted:

(a) at eight-hourly intervals for traffic with Cerrito, near Montevideo, the nearest cable link with Britain. Intended for commercial traffic, this service was also used for urgent naval messages, Uruguay turning a 'blind eye' to this breach of her neutrality if they were disguised as being to and from the Governor of the Falklands.

(b) at 2100 daily to pass commercial traffic direct to and from the GPO station at Dorchester.

(c) at 2200 daily to pass naval traffic direct to and from Whitehall.

To overcome the delays of 12 hours or more which this limited service imposed on signals from the Admiralty and from the C-in-C South Atlantic at Freetown (whose traffic had to be routed via Whitehall), HM ships (which normally maintained W/T silence so as to avoid disclosing their positions) listened every four hours for messages broadcast on VLF (16kcs) by the high-power GPO–

Admiralty Rugby transmitter, in addition to keeping continuous watch on the Falklands broadcast.

Signals from HM ships, including the Commodore South American Division, were normally transmitted to Freetown or Simonstown W/T stations for onward routing. But since a frequency as low as 6mcs was allotted for this purpose, communication could seldom be established with either during daylight hours. To overcome the delays which this involved, HM ships in South American waters could, in an emergency, establish direct touch with each other on the Falkland Islands broadcast frequency. (On December 13, 1939, Commodore Harwood used this method to order the *Cumberland* to leave the Falklands and join him off the Plate.)

Appreciating the considerable delays inherent in the Falklands–Cerrito link, the British Naval Attaché improvised a receiving station in the Embassy at Buenos Aires to keep a constant listening watch on the Falklands broadcast and on the ship-shore H/F frequency to Freetown and Simonstown. This was of special value after the battle of the Plate when the British Minister's diplomacy depended on up-to-the-minute knowledge of Commodore Harwood's intentions.

In common with all HM ships, those in South American waters kept a listening watch on the commercial frequency of 500kcs, notably for distress messages, including those reporting attack by an enemy raider in which RRR replaced SOS (*e.g.* 'RRR RRR 19° 15′ south, 05° 05′ east *Doric Star* gunned pocket-battleship').

During the battle of the Plate the British cruisers were in direct touch with each other by W/T on 350kcs, except during the periods when the aerials of the *Ajax* and *Exeter* were brought down by gunfire, and had to be replaced by jury ones. The *Ajax* and *Achilles* also used W/T for concentrating their gunfire, which was effective during the first phase of the battle, until from 0646 onwards this link, using Type 45, failed.

In 1939 all naval aircraft used morse for communication with HM ships. Because aircraft transmitters were of low power, planes on reconnaissance flights were allocated a special medium frequency so that they would not suffer jamming by ships' higher powered sets. And because spotting aircraft needed to make their reports immediately if they were to be of use, each ship was allocated a high frequency (approx 4mcs) which was reserved for this purpose. The *Ajax*'s Seafox failed initially to establish communication because, in the haste with which the plane was launched after fire had been opened, its set was tuned to the reconnaissance frequency (230kcs). Not until the observer retuned to the spotting frequency (3·8mcs) on which the *Ajax* was listening, were his fall of shot and other reports well received.

The *Admiral Graf Spee*'s W/T organisation was both simpler and more tenuous. Her only link was Nauen, near Berlin, which broadcast messages to her and other raiders using high power on three high frequencies simultaneously; and which she could call at any time when she needed to pass a signal to the German Admiralty or to a supply ship of sufficient importance to justify breaking W/T silence.

Like the *Ajax*, the *Graf Spee* used medium frequency W/T to communicate with her reconnaissance aircraft. She also kept watch on 500kcs, especially when closing a potential victim, so as to be ready to jam any attempt to transmit a raider distress signal.

The *Graf Spee* had the advantage of a special unit which monitored transmissions to Allied merchant ships from which, especially after seizing the Admiralty code from the ss *Newton Beech*, Langsdorff gained useful intelligence.

APPENDIX THIRTEEN

Radar

Paralleling the Royal Air Force's invention and development of Radar (Radio Detection and Ranging, initially known as RDF= Reflection Direction Finding) in the five years before World War II, as a device for detecting and giving warning of enemy aircraft approaching Britain, the Royal Navy equipped the cruiser *Sheffield* in August 1938 with its first ship-borne radar set, Type 79. Transmitting on a metric wavelength, this had an effective range against aircraft at 10000 feet of some 120 miles. It could also, but only incidentally, detect surface craft out to about 8 miles. Type 79 was also fitted in the battleship *Rodney* at the end of the same year, but only a small handful of other ships had been similarly equipped a year later—and these did not include the *Achilles*, *Ajax* or *Exeter*. Nor, by the time the battle of the River Plate was fought, had the Royal Navy developed Radar for any other purpose.

Germany 'discovered' Radar almost simultaneously with the British, but without appreciating its prime value for detecting aircraft. The German Navy developed its first *De Tet-Gerät* (*i.e. Deutsches Technisches Gerät*=German Technical Equipment) which operated initially on 50cms and later 80cms, for gunnery ranging in time for the first set to be fitted in the *Graf Spee*, with a 'mattress' aerial on the foreside of the control tower, in 1938. Its range was, however, limited to 16000 yards so that it was only of value in low visibility or at night. In the battle of the Plate the *Graf Spee* had to rely on her long-base rangefinders, of which one was installed aloft in the control tower. These, as in the ships of the High Seas Fleet in World War I, were more accurate than any in the British Navy.

APPENDIX FOURTEEN

British Shell Hits on the Graf Spee

Note

Nos 2, 3 and 15 are 8in shell hits by HMS *Exeter*, the remainder are 6in hits by HMS *Ajax* and HMNZS *Achilles*.

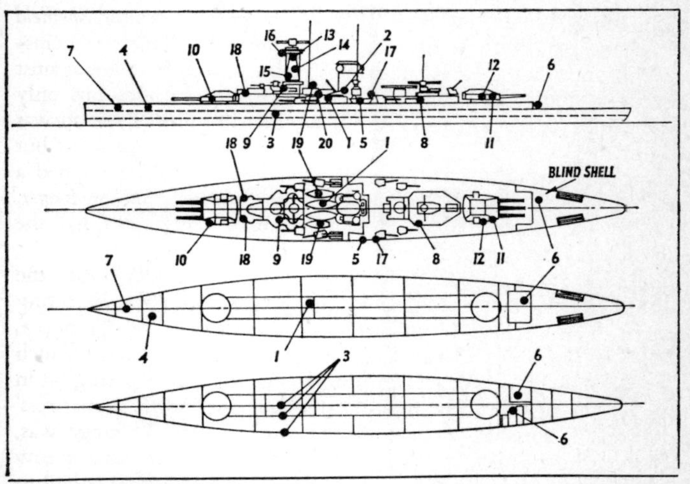

Diagram 6. Positions of British shell hits on the *Admiral Graf Spee*

APPENDIX FIFTEEN

British Honours and Awards

Knight Commander of the Order of the Bath

Commodore Henry Harwood (who also received immediate promotion to rear-admiral)

Companion of the Order of the Bath

Captain F. S. Bell	(*Exeter*)
Captain W. E. Parry	(*Achilles*)
Captain C. H. L. Woodhouse	(*Ajax*)

Distinguished Service Order

Commander D. H. Everett	(*Ajax*)
Commander R. R. Graham	(*Exeter*)
Commander D. M. L. Neame	(*Achilles*)
Commander (E) C. E. Simms	(*Exeter*)
Lieutenant R. E. Washbourn	(*Achilles*)
Lieutenant I. D. De'ath, RM	(*Ajax*)

Distinguished Service Cross

Lieutenant-Commander D. P. Dreyer	(*Ajax*)
Lieutenant-Commander R. B. Jennings*	(*Exeter*)
Lieutenant-Commander C. J. Smith*	(*Exeter*)
Lieutenant G. G. Cowburn	(*Achilles*)
Lieutenant E. D. G. Lewin	(*Ajax*)
Lieutenant N. K. Tod	(*Ajax*)
Lieutenant A. E. Toase, RM	(*Exeter*)
Surgeon-Lieutenant C. G. Hunter	(*Achilles*)
Surgeon-Lieutenant R. W. G. Lancashire	(*Exeter*)
Midshipman A. Cameron	(*Exeter*)
Midshipman R. W. D. Don	(*Exeter*)
Gunner R. C. Biggs	(*Ajax*)

* Who also received immediate promotion to Commander.

Gunner H. T. Burchall (*Achilles*)
Gunner E. J. Watts (*Achilles*)
Warrant Engineer A. P. Monk (*Ajax*)
Warrant Shipwright F. H. T. Panter (*Ajax*)
Warrant Shipwright C. E. Rendle (*Exeter*)

Conspicuous Gallantry Medal
Able Seaman G. Guilliam (*Exeter*)
Stoker P. O'Brien (*Exeter*)
Marine W. A. Russell (*Exeter*)
Sergeant S. J. Trimble, RM (*Achilles*)

Distinguished Service Medal
Able Seaman A. J. Ball (*Exeter*)
Engineroom Artificer F. L. Bond (*Exeter*)
Chief Petty Officer W. G. Boniface (*Achilles*)
Chief Petty Officer Telegraphist W. L. Brewer (*Achilles*)
Marine T. S. Buckley (*Ajax*)
Master-at-Arms S. A. Carter (*Exeter*)
Petty Officer H. V. Chalkeley (*Exeter*)
Sergeant R. G. Cook, RM (*Ajax*)
Leading Seaman L. C. Curd (*Ajax*)
Sick Berth Attendant E. T. Dakin (*Exeter*)
Chief Mechanician W. G. Dorling (*Ajax*)
Boy A. M. Dorset (*Achilles*)
Petty Officer A. E. Fuller (*Ajax*)
Petty Officer C. H. C. Gorton (*Ajax*)
Able Seaman H. H. Gould (*Achilles*)
Shipwright D. Graham (*Ajax*)
Petty Officer W. E. Green (*Exeter*)
Petty Officer C. F. Hallas (*Exeter*)
Petty Officer W. R. Headon (*Achilles*)
Petty Officer J. W. Hill (*Ajax*)
Chief Mechanician L. Hood (*Achilles*)
Electrical Artificer J. W. Jenkins (*Ajax*)
Joiner F. Knight (*Exeter*)
Able Seaman R. D. Macey (*Ajax*)
Engineroom Artificer J. McGarry (*Exeter*)
Able Seaman R. McClarnan (*Ajax*)
Chief Yeoman of Signals L. C. Martinson (*Achilles*)

Petty Officer A. Maycock	(*Achilles*)
Stoker J. L. Minhinett	(*Exeter*)
Stoker F. E. Monk	(*Ajax*)
Stoker R. C. Perry	(*Ajax*)
Engineroom Artificer T. G. Phillips	(*Exeter*)
Sick Berth Chief Petty Officer C. D. Pope	(*Exeter*)
Ordinary Seaman I. T. L. Rodgers	(*Achilles*)
Chief Mechanician J. A. Rooskey	(*Exeter*)
Chief Ordnance Artificer G. H. Sampson	(*Achilles*)
Sergeant F. T. Saunders, RM	(*Achilles*)
Able Seaman E. V. Sherley	(*Achilles*)
Petty Officer S. J. Smith	(*Exeter*)
Plumber G. E. Smith	(*Exeter*)
Leading Airman E. A. Shoesmith	(*Exeter*)
Chief Stoker W. J. Wain	(*Achilles*)
Sergeant A. B. Wilde, RM	(*Exeter*)
Stoker B. Wood	(*Ajax*)
Cook A. G. Young	(*Achilles*)

Many other officers and men of all three ships were 'mentioned in despatches'.

APPENDIX SIXTEEN

British Merchant Ships Sunk by the Graf Spee

Name	*Tons Gross*	*Year built*	*Owner or Manager*	*Master*	*Fate*
Clement	5051	1934	Booth SS Co Ltd	F. C. P. Harris	Sunk 30.9.39
Newton Beech	4651	1925	J. Ridley Son & Tulley	J. Robinson	Captured 5.10.39 Sunk 9.10.39
Ashlea	4222	1929	J. Morrison & Son	C. Pottinger	Sunk 7.10.39
Huntsman	8196	1921	Thomas & James Harrison	A. H. Brown	Captured 10.10.39 Sunk 17.10.39
Trevanion	5299	1937	Hain SS Co	J. M. Edwards	Sunk 22.10.39
Africa Shell	706	1939	Shell Co of East Africa	P. Dove	Sunk 15.11.39
Doric Star	10086	1921	Blue Star Line	W. Stubbs	Sunk 2.12.39
Tairoa	7983	1920	Shaw Savill & Albion Co	W. B. S. Starr	Sunk 3.12.39
Streonshalh	3895	1928	Headlam and Sons	J. J. Robinson	Sunk 7.12.39
Total	50089				

APPENDIX SEVENTEEN

Tailpiece

How the news reached Omsk and Tomsk

'Nobody would dare say that the loss of a German battleship [*sic*] is a brilliant victory for the British fleet. This is rather a demonstration, unprecedented in history, of the impotence of the British. Upon the morning of 13 December the battleship started an artillery duel with the *Exeter*, and within a few minutes obliged the cruiser to withdraw from the action. According to the latest information the *Exeter* sank near the Argentine coast, en route for the Falkland Islands.'

(*The Soviet Newspaper* Red Fleet, *December 31, 1939*.)

Select Bibliography

History

Action This Day. Admiral of the Fleet Sir Philip Vian.

Battle of the River Plate. Commander A. B. Campbell.

Battle of the River Plate: an Account of Events before, during and after the Action. British Admiralty.

Battle of the River Plate. Dudley Pope.

Battle of the River Plate. Lord Strabolgi.

Despatch of 30 December 1939, published in London Gazette, *17 June 1947*. Rear-Admiral Sir Henry Harwood.

Drama of Graf Spee *and the Battle of the Plate*. Sir Eugen Millington-Drake.

Einsatz der Schweren Kriegsmarineeinheiten. Captain G. Bidlingmaier.

Graf Spee *1939: The German Story*. British Admiralty (restricted circulation).

I was Graf Spee's *Prisoner*. Captain Patrick Dove.

Panzerschiff Admiral Graf Spee. Commander F. W. Rasenack.

Naval Policy between the Wars, Vol. I. Stephen Roskill.

Second World War, Vol. I. Winston S. Churchill.

Struggle for the Sea. Grand Admiral Raedar.

Swastika at Sea: the Struggle and Destruction of the German Navy, 1939–1945. C. D. Bekker.

Un Episodio de la Segunda Guerra Mundial. General Alfredo R. Campos.

Uruguayan Blue Book. (English translation published by Hutchinson, 1940).

War at Sea, Vol. I. Captain S. W. Roskill, RN.

Technical

Brassey's Naval Annual.

Die Deutschen Kriegschiffe. E. Groner.

German Surface Vessels. H. T. Lenton.

German Warships of World War II. J. C. Taylor.

Janes Fighting Ships.

Schlachtschiffe und Schlachtkreuzer, 1905–1970. Siegfried Breyer.

Warships of World War II. H. T. Lenton and J. Colledge.

Index